how to pick WINNING HORSES

Published by
Melvin Powers
WILSHIRE BOOK COMPANY
12015 Sherman Road
No. Hollywood, California 91605
Telephone: (213) 875-1711 / (818) 983-1105

Printed by

HAL LEIGHTON PRINTING COMPANY
P.O. Box 3952
North Hollywood, California 91605
Telephone: (213) 983-1105

Published by arrangement with Citadel Press
(a subsidiary of Lyle Stuart, Inc.)

Published by Citadel Press, Inc.
A subsidiary of Lyle Stuart, Inc.
120 Enterprise Ave., Secaucus, N. J. 07094
In Canada: George J. McLeod Limited
73 Bathurst St., Toronto 2B, Ontario
Manufactured in the United States of America

ISBN-87980-266-9

CONTENTS

1. The Racing Secretary

Let's set the tone of this book right at the starting gate by admitting that only some five percent of the hoss players are able to select winning horses consistently. And while we're being honest about that, let's go farther and admit this same percentage will hold true in any form of endeavor you care to mention.

If a hundred people suddenly decide they'll go into the gas station business, only five of them will make a success of it. If a hundred start grocery stores, ninety-five of them will fail.

So hoss playing isn't an exception, but that needn't scare you off. You've already started in the right direction by picking up this book, for the successful five percent in any line know their groundwork. And they know the angles and gimmicks that spell the difference between success and failure. And that, fellers and gals, is what we're going to discuss in the following chapters.

Maybe you've already made a sufficient study of thoroughbred racing to have a vague feeling that there *is* a way to win if you could only come up with the magic formula. Or maybe you're already convinced all this yak-yak about nobody being able to beat the races is the McCoy. If you're reading this for laughs, stick around and be convinced.

Or perhaps you're a newcomer to the turf who doesn't rightly know which end of a horse eats, but you've heard talk about how horse racing has supplanted baseball as the national spectator sport. And how could forty million horse fans be wrong?

Whatever your reason for picking up this book; whether you have a yen to make turf speculation your life's work; or just gather in an honest bob or two on your day off. No matter what you need or where you need it, it's here.

So while I've got my neck out, I might as well make it a wire-to-wire effort.

The races *can* be beat.

With sufficient grounding in the art of selection, and the mathematics of turf speculation, *you too can beat them.* It can be done, in fact, even if you're one of those people who can never learn to handicap. Some people just never get to the stage where they can select a hot dog at a weenie roast.

So now that I'm all the way out on a limb, it's up to me to prove the limb will hold. Okay, pull up a chair and let's get started.

So far all we know for sure is that it's not easy to pick winners. But what makes it so hard? It seems to me that before we can make an intelligent bid to join the exclusive society of the five-percenters, we've got to understand what makes selecting winning horses so tough.

No, it's not bum racing luck, or the fact that you haven't been holding your ears right. And it's not because the races are run the night before in a smoke-filled room along Shed Row. There is no inside crowd that manipulates the results.

But there is one man at every track who is paid a nice fat salary to make it rough for you and me.

He is the *racing secretary*.

It may sound contradictory, but for the most part he is a very nice gentleman who is just trying to do a good job for his boss, the track management. The only way he can please his boss is by giving you and me a hard time, and if he doesn't succeed in this, chances are he won't be doing business at the same stand come next meeting.

Each track, of course, has it's own racing secretary, though many of them serve at more than one track when no conflict in dates arises, and they are about as close to the racing picture as a man can get. These gentlemen are horsemen through and through, frequently ex-stable owners or trainers, born in a feed box and teethed on a bit ring.

It is their function, and avowed purpose, to card races in which each and every horse entered will have an equal chance. It is the cherished dream of every racing secretary to some day balance a field so skillfully that the race will culminate in a "blanket" finish. Horses, being high-strung, temperamental flesh and blood, are not very often cooperative with the racing secretary's aims, but the more close finishes he can arrange, the more certain he is to be rehired for a repeat performance.

I hate to tell you this, fellers and gals, but these otherwise nice gentlemen don't care a whoop whether you and I make a buck or not. All they're concerned with is tight finishes involving the most possible horses, and the more successful they are at this, the harder it is going to be for me, and for you, to point up any one nag as a mortal cinch.

Is it any wonder, then, that only roughly thirty percent of the anticipated winners actually get the job done, taken as a national average? Is it so hard to understand, once we understand what the racing secretary is up to, that a lot of longshots get home free?

It sort of reminds me of the story they tell along any Shed Row, or in most any Backstretch Café where horsemen are wont to gather, about the two stewards at Gulfstream Park, where Racing Secretary Horace Wade did a particularly able job of creating thrilling stretch duels. The two stewards in question were a conscientious pair. It was their habit to handicap a race thoroughly before it was run so as to have a pretty fair working knowledge of what to expect in the actual running to come.

After a particularly tedious study session, the reaction seemed to be utter frustration.

"What do you think, Ed?" one of the stewards said. "Looks kind of tight to me."

"John," Ed said, "this race is set up so dad-blamed tight there isn't a dag-nabbed hide in it that can run first, second, or third."

All right, so there's no point trying to dodge the inevitable question. Why should the track management want it this way? Wouldn't the powers be better pleased if favorite after favorite won, thus making the largest segment of cash customers happy?

Look at it this way. Horse racing is a spectacular show. The track management is marketing thrills, color and excitement. They know that not even a winning parimutuel pasteboard clutched in our hot little hand can equal the thrill, color and excitement, for *everybody* present, of a riot of jockey silks on a closely bunched field of thoroughbreds charging at the wire in a wide-open race which could be taken by a nose or a whisker by any one of those straining contestants.

You can bet the bottom of your pocket the management knows that if they can send us home weak from spent emotions and hoarse from screaming field after field down to the wire, we'll be back. And it won't be because a certain number of favorites did or did not substantiate our peculiar genius as handicappers. They know that by giving us clean and exciting racing, they won't have to worry about the gate or the mutuel "handle."

Believe me, the track management knows exactly what it's doing when it pays big money for the best racing secretary it can get, one who will make the races it offers to the public as unpredictable as is humanly possible.

Some of the more cynical of us will no doubt take the view that the crowds gravitate to the tracks mainly because of the legalized parimutuel wagering, and there can be no question about the drawing strength of this inducement. But it does not explain the phenomenal rise in popularity of the Sport of Kings in recent years. Even before the advent of the parimutuel method of wagering, there was betting at the tracks through the picturesque bookmakers of that era. If you wanted to speculate on the outcome of a hoss race, action has always been at hand. But it has been only in recent years that track management has come to recognize the necessity of catering to the intrepid two-buck improver of the breed. Reforms have been instituted to protect him against larcenous practices. More and better seating has been provided for his comfort, and escalators for his convenience. Until comparatively recent years the races were run solely for the horsemen, and if the fans didn't like the conditions as they found them around the hoss plants, they could stay away—which they did, in droves.

There is still room for improvement, such as the ridiculous charges made by the caterers (fifteen cents for a five-cent coke, for instance, and fifteen cents for a cup of mediocre coffee—plus one-cent tax in Florida, yet.) But for the most part the day of the fan has arrived, and with it skyrocketing attendance and mutuel handle.

So there's more behind it than our eagerness to risk a coupla bucks on the outcome of a hoss race. We'll have more to say about this later. Right now what we want to know is how the racing secretary goes about making the races hard to beat, for if we understand why and how he operates, we enhance our chances of outsmarting him. And that's what we're going to have to do if we expect to pick up a bob or two at the track.

The racing secretary eats and sleeps with the Scale of Weights. This Scale is the basis for regulating the number of pounds, or impost, each age group must carry at certain seasons of the year. And it allows for concessions to fillies and mares when competing against males and geldings.

In January, for instance, when all thoroughbreds automatically become one year older regardless of the date they were foaled (That's right. January 1st is *every* thoroughbred's birthday), a three-year-old should be granted, according to the Scale, a weight concession so large, when and if he is asked to compete against older horses, as to make such a race practically impossible to card if adhered to. However, during the ensuing months as the three-year-old fills out and gains strength, this concession is gradually reduced until by late autumn he is running on nearly equal terms with the four-year-old. Also the five-pound allowance for fillies and mares when racing against horses, colts and geldings is reduced to three pounds in the fall of the year.

The purpose of the Scale, of course, is to endeavor to equalize the various age groups, and females, so that all shall have an equal chance to collect a purse.

Obviously, since no two horses are exactly alike, the Scale is merely the general rule for impost assignment. For the racing secretary, it is the starting point. Working from the Scale, he writes the *condition book*. In this, the secretary provides for certain allowances and/or penalties depending upon whether the horses involved have won within a certain period of time; or how many races they have won during this period; or how much money they have earned since such-and-such a date. From the stipulated conditions, it is up to the trainer to decide whether or not he cares to enter his beastie.

Only in the Handicap races does the racing secretary assign weights directly. Here also, his basis is the Scale, to which he adds or subtracts poundage according to recent proven ability. In the Handicap, definitely, the highest weighted horse is the best horse in the opinion of the racing secretary. By penalizing him with high weight, the secretary hopes to "bring him back" to an even footing with the light-weight of the group and those variously weighted in between, so that all might have an equal chance to win. Mostly, he is adamant about his assignments, though there might be times when, in order to get some special drawing card, such as Nashua, he is forced to be politic. I mention Nashua especially because his connections, during his final months of competition, made it quite clear they would not race him at more than 130 pounds. Thus he ran in some pretty poor company with what amounted to a feather.

These occurrences are comparatively rare, however, and the experienced player does not speculate on this type of contest anyhow, since it would be foolhardy to bet against such an outstanding performer and equally foolish to risk one's hard-gotten cash on him in the hope of collecting what must amount to little more than a pittance for the effort.

The only time I can recall that I bet against such an outstanding performer was some years ago at Santa Anita during the time when the great mare, Busher, was showing them all the way home. It was a seven-furlong affair and, under the circumstances, it looked to me as though it might be a little short for Busher. The circumstances, according to my figures, were embodied in a capable sprinter by the name of Quick Reward. As usual, everybody chunked it in on Busher, and she did give them a magnificent run for their money. But it wasn't quite good enough to catch Quick Reward. He paid thirty-six bucks and some odd change for each two-buck pasteboard.

To get back to the racing secretary, he writes his condition book weeks in advance of a meeting, and the horsemen thumb their copies dog-eared trying to find races where one or more of their horses might enjoy a slight advantage under the Conditions. And while they're thumbing through the book, you can be sure nobody loves the racing secretary. Every horseman along Shed Row is of the unshakeable opinion that the so-and-so secretary has written the book for the sole purpose of assuring his personal insovency.

So, let's you and I take a look at a few of the Conditions and see just what kind of skulduggery the secretary has been guilty of. Though few fans seem to be aware of it, and fewer still ever bother to read them, they are made available to us at the heading of each set of past performances in the *Daily Racing Form,* and the *Telegraph,* and are reprinted in the program we buy at the track. This alone should be the tip-off as to their importance.

Here, taken at random, are the Conditions for an Allowance race:-

6 FURLONGS. Purse, $4,500. 3 year olds, non-winners two races other than maiden or claiming at any time. Allowances. Weight 122 lbs. Non-winners of $7,500 allowed 3 lbs; two races since October 20, 6 lbs; $3,000 at any time or a race since November 25, 9 lbs; a race since October 2, 12 lbs.; (Claiming and maiden races not considered.) Maidens, 12 lbs.

Now there's a real stinker for you. The Man must have worked up a headache over that one.

Since the race is open to three-year-olds only, the scale weight is 122 pounds, and weight concessions are offered for failure to have earned a certain amount of money, or failure to have won (other than in maiden or claiming races) within a certain prescribed time.

In the following chapter, we're going to spend some time and space analyzing Conditions so the fan will understand their importance, and will know after studying the Conditions for a given race in which direction to look with the best chance of coming up with a winner. For now it is enough if I have been able to impress upon you that the yardstick for the racing secretary is weight.

Naturally, the owners and trainers are extremely weight conscious, too. There is an old expression among horsemen that says, "Weight will stop a freight train." What it means, of course, is that no matter how good a horse is, he can be slowed down if his impost is heavy enough. We'll have more to say about the weight factor later in the text, too, but for now if we understand that the racing secretary and the horsemen consider it all-important, we have made progress in the right direction.

This emphasis on weight, almost to the exclusion of the other factors, is the Achilles' heel by which we can subdue the guy who's making it tough for us.

2. The Conditions

Since the condition book is the bible of racing secretary and horsemen alike, it is amazing how few fans ever read the conditions for a given race before attempting to make selections for same. How they can ignore the thing which is the backbone of the race they hope to beat is to me one of those unexplainable phenomena one constantly encounters around the hoss tracks.

True, the language used is quaint and often cryptic to the uninitiated. But it makes good sense to those who learn to interpret it, for understanding the conditions under which the race will be run often points up the most likely angle to use to isolate the most probable winner.

So, in this chapter we're going to analyze conditions in the hope that it will become the habit of the fan to always first learn the nature of the race before attempting to predict the outcome.

For instance, one or both of the Daily Double races at any man's track are usually rather unpredictable betting mediums. This is true because of the class of competition and the nature of the conditions, which are usually pretty loose in order to encourage the owners to enter their doubtful charges. In Chapter 1 we presented a fairly complicated set of conditions. Cmpare these with the conditions for the first race of the Daily Double pair, taken at random from the *Form*.

1¼ MILES (Track Record, etc.) Purse, $3500. 4-year-olds and upwards. Claiming. 120 lbs. Claiming price, $3500. Winners in 1956, 2 lbs. additional for each race won.

In this race, the age group is stated (4-year-olds and up), and the general class of the competition controlled by the $3500 claiming tag. That it is bound to attract a pretty sorry lot is attested to by the weight penalty for having won in 1956. No 1956 winners accepted, so we have a full field of contestants that have not yet demonstrated their ability to win in 1956. Present form then could be the tip-off here.

The second half of the Daily Double on this same day was an allowance race at six furlongs for "non-winners of two races." In other words, they are all only once removed from the lowly Maiden classification. The weight stipulated is 122 pounds with 4 pounds allowed off for those that have not earned $3250. Since none of them had earned this much, the weight was automatically lowered to 118 pounds. This, then, since it is a sprint, should best lend itself to a speed analysis.

It so happened that a big fat longshot won the first race, though his steadily improving form over his past four races was right there for everybody to see. The second race was won by a speed merchant of such superior quality that he was made the even money favorite.

It will be noticed the more the student becomes familiar with stipulated conditions, that no direct reference is ever made to speed. Yet speed is a direct line on class, and can tell us when nothing else will, whether or not the horse we are considering is in good form. We'll go into this more thoroughly later under handicapping factors. For now let it be sufficient to say that speed is a very useful commodity, and one which is vastly underrated by too many selectors.

Here are the conditions for one of the better types of claiming races:-

6 FURLONGS. Purse, $4500. 4-year-olds and upward. Claiming. 124 lbs. Claiming price, $15,000. Non-winners of three races

since November 10 allowed 3 lbs.; two races since November 10, or a race since January 16, 5 lbs.; a race since November 26, 7 lbs.

As could be expected, this set of conditions attracted a wide divergence of competition, not only from the better claimer ranks but also from the allowance, handicap and stakes branches of horsedom. Obviously, the angle here is going to be true class plus the necessary evidence of present sharp condition, or form, for it must be understood no horse can demonstrate his true class, or speed, or consistency if he is off form. He must be at or near peak racing edge or else he is certain to be beaten by a lesser animal which *is* in peak form.

In this particular race, the eventual winner received the 7 lb. weight allowance because he had not won since November 26, but there was plenty of evidence that he was sharp. He not only had the fastest recent race, but his speed ratings had increased steadily over his last three races. On top of this, he was three to one the highest class. He won easily.

Now here is an example of the kind of thing which should never be carded in the early months of any year:-

MILE AND SEVENTY YARDS. Purse, $900. 3- and 4-year-olds. Maidens. Claiming. 3-year-olds, 113 lbs; 4-year-olds, 118 lbs. Claiming price $1500.

This race was carded on February 2, 1956, a time of the year when the Scale of Weights makes it practically impossible to equitably weight the two age groups. In other words, with the four-year-olds carrying 118 pounds, the three-year-olds should come in at about 80 pounds, but this set of conditions requires the four-year-olds to give the younger horses only five pounds. Needless to say, the race was won by a four-year-old, but the fan would do well to avoid any race for three-year-olds and older until the fall of the year. To state it another way, three-year-olds should race against three-year-olds for at least the first six months of the year, and better yet, until about September. By September, the three-year-old will have attained sufficient growth and strength to be able to look the older horses in the eye, other factors being equal, of course.

Now here is a plain claimer with none of the allowance features written in:

> 5½ FURLONGS. Purse, $900. 4-year-olds and upwards, non-winners since September 1. Claiming. 4-year 116 lbs; older, 118 lbs. Claiming price, $1500.

Since there is only two pounds difference in weight between the two age classifications, the thing to look for here is a possible advantage in claiming class, provided, of course, peak form is indicated. For instance, in this affair, a five-year-old gelding by the name of Oalo has been racing in allowances and $5000 claimers. Obviously he is taking a dive in class to enter this $1500 claimer. But he had not raced since April of 1955, and while he has been working satisfactorily, there is no reason for us to believe he is sharp enough to win at first asking.

On the other hand, there is a cheapie named Ha Whoa that has been running recently at this track at today's claiming price. He has no class advantage but his last two races show he is approaching peak form. He closed resolutely in his last, less than a week previously, to finish in-the-money, beaten only a length and a half. In his next to last race, he was on the pace into the stretch, but was a little short in the run to the wire. The pattern of these two recent races proves conclusively that he is about to hit his peak.

Oalo's superior class could not quite overcome Ha Whoa's sharp form. The cheap one won it, and the classier Oalo ran second.

Now let's clear up another general point before we go any

farther. It will probably be felt by the system player that studying conditions is strictly for the handicapper, the analyst. While the importance of the conditions cannot be underestimated by the conscientious handicapper and analyst, this is also true to only a slightly lesser degree for the system player. A one-system player, while infinitely better off than the "my-mother-told-me-to-take-this-one" school of blind stabbers, is still not giving himself the best of it. He is bound to have noticed that his system does better some days than others, and works better at some tracks than others. In fact, it is quite possible to have a system that is hotter than a pistol at one track and won't work at all at another.

What's the answer? The difference in the conditions set up by the different racing secretaries. If a system player were to land on a hot system, and were to use it only at those tracks serviced by the same secretary, he would find he would get amazingly uniform results at all tracks so serviced.

If you have the mistaken idea that all secretaries function basically alike, take a look at these. The first is a set of conditions for an allowance race at Gulfstream Park, the Horace Wade variety:

MILE AND 70 YARDS (Swaps-April 14, 1956-1:39⅗-4-130) THE BONNIE SCOTLAND. Purse $4000. 3-year-olds which have never won three races. Allowances. Weight, 122 lbs. Non-winners of $3,250 allowed 3 lbs.; of $2,600, 6 lbs.; of a race of any value, 9 lbs. (Maiden, claiming, or optional races not considered.) Maidens, 12 lbs.

And here's an allowance at Sunshine Park, authored by Jack Klucina:

MILE AND 70 YARDS (Deep Thought-Jan. 21, 1956-1:41⅘-4-116) Purse, $1,100. 3- and 4-year-olds that have never won two races. Allowances. 3-year-olds, 114 lbs.; 4-year-olds, 120 lbs. Non winners in 1957 allowed 3 lbs.; September 15, 5 lbs.

Even the inexperienced selector should not expect the same system or the same handicapping analysis to point up the most likely winner in both of these. And yet the one-system player and the inflexible handicapper expect just that and will curse foul racing luck and crooked manipulation when their results are less than satisfactory.

The answer for the system player is, of course, to avail himself of several good systems, let's say a class system, a speed system, and a consistency system as a bare minimum spread. Then he must become conditions-conscious and use the system which is applicable.

Later on in this book, we will present a dozen or so good systems. From these the student should be able to find the ones best suited to his use.

The budding handicapper-analyst, on the other hand, must learn to govern an elastic and flexible handicapping procedure by what he has just read in the conditions for the race immediately under consideration. The conditions should tell him what value or stress to put on what factor or factors. Once he has learned to analyze and understand the conditions, the rest of his work will be greatly simplified, and his win percentage correspondingly higher.

It's not as difficult as it may seem. Neither can it be wholly absorbed from one exposure. If you want to be a virtuoso, you must be willing to practice. If a thing is worth doing at all, it's worth doing well. This could be said to be especially true where it has a direct affect on one's solvency.

So get some back issues of the *Form* or *Telegraph*, study the conditions until you think you see the best way to handle it, then compare your selection with the results given in the next day's paper. Make a workout of your progress. Soon, you will begin to note definite improvement. Operation Red should turn into Operation Black.

3. Class

One hears a lot of gabble around the hoss tracks about *class*. Like the weather, however, nobody does anything about it— nothing constructive or particularly intelligent, that is. Most of the fans who talk most about class can't even define it, much less use it to advantage.

In order to understand class and its use and value as a handicapping factor, we'd best do a wrecking job first on some of the most prevalent misconceptions. After disposing of the superstitions, contradictions, and plain hogwash which passes for class delineation, we're going to have something really constructive and useable to offer the selector. We will put class on a monetary basis, which is the only way it should be of any interest to the budding speculator.

First, let's see what's wrong with the general class picture as one encounters it at the spectator level of the horse factories.

BLOODLINES

Unless the fan is anticipating an appearance on a quiz show in which his category will be horse genealogy, he'd better leave blood lines to the breeders. From the speculators' viewpoint, bloodlines come under the heading of facts not worth knowing.

I can almost hear the howls of protest, but don't worry. I'm not going to leave my contention unsupported. And if you still want to back bloodlines with hard cash after we're through—well, it's your money.

Let's just grab up a *Form*. Here's a Rosemont gelding. He's earned $375.00 in eighteen starts. And here's a mare who has Reigh Count amoung her antecedants. She has earned $1,150 dollars in thirteen tries. That's class? And there's a Challenge Me filly—$2,280 in nineteen races. Here's one by First Fiddle-Seaway, by Man O'War. The earnings here were $4,475 in twenty starts.

Man O'War was considered a pretty handy sort a few years back, and so was First Fiddle, best remembered as the Grey Ghost, or Mr. Out-Of-The-Clouds.

Sure, Man O'War and First Fiddle had class. They were champs, not because of their bloodlines but because they proved their class at the racing wars, something many of their get have been unable to do in spite of their bloodlines.

Mind you, I have nothing against bloodlines provided they have been substantiated by enough successes in competition to prove that some of the ancestral glitter has, in fact, rubbed off on them. On the other hand, if I decide to play a good hard hitting hide off his record, it doesn't matter in the slightest who his pappy or his grandpappy was. His antecedents may have been wholly devoid of class, but I know this one has a touch of class by the way he has been performing.

There have been some good ones come up from the ranks, so to speak. And the ones who have started out in life as the get of illustrious parentage and have proven monumental flops as racers are legion.

So if your selections must be glorified by bloodlines, make

sure they also have performance lines to match before you take the rubber band off your bank roll.

CLAIMING TAGS AS A CLASS COMPARISON

There are those fans around every man's track who seem to think the price tag a nag carries is a clear indication of his quality and thus his ability as a racer. There was, in fact, a time when this was more nearly true than it is today. Perhaps this is why the idea still persists. In recent years, however, the tendency has been to shift from one claiming level to another with such frequency that the true level of a horse becomes obscured if not wholly obliterated. And the introduction of the "optional claimer" a few years back has helped to clarify this situation not at all. In fact, there are those who claim that identification via claiming tag went out with the advent of the optional claimer.

In the old-fashioned claiming race, an owner risked the loss of his horse to a halterman at the stipulated claiming price. Period. In the optional claimer, the owner has the option of either entering his horse to be claimed or entering him not to be claimed. If an owner does not want to enter his horse to be claimed, his horse must meet the "optional conditions" set up by the racing secretary, and if his horse should win this race, then he cannot re-enter him in this same class of optional claimer except as eligible to be claimed.

This allows for certain maneuverings totally confusing to the average fan, but this same fan will continue to classify his selections via the claiming tag route. Here's the sort of pit the inexperienced fan falls into:

The 4th at Hialeah on February 2, 1956 was at 1⅛ MILES (turf) (Mackville-Feb. 20, 1954-1:49⅘-5-119) Purse $4,000. 3-year-olds. Claiming. 124 lbs. Claiming price, $8,000. Non-winners overturf allowed 3 lbs.; two races since November 26, 6 lbs.; 3 lbs. for each $500 to $7,000.

Three of the contestants were entered at the minimum claiming tag of $7,000, four were entered at the maximum of $8,000, and six were entered at $7,500. Ray's Blue Man raced at $10,000 last time out. He had won for a $5,000 tag at Hawthorne six months previously and had won an allowance at Sportsman three months previously. One wonders what the owner was trying to prove. Certainly Ray's Blue Man was no $10,000 horse, nor was he an $8,000 horse. But to the inexperienced it appeared that the colt was being dropped from ten to eight thousand for a melon cutting.

Hicks Beach had been raced variously and without rhyme or reason at tags varying from $3,000 to $7,500 and won none of them. Greek Sword from $4,500 to $9,500 with a win at $5,000. Yeoni had won at $6,500; Elliott's Gem at $4,500 and $5,000. Little Pharo had won only a Maiden race. Rockport had won at $7,500 at Tropical. Simmi J. had won at $7,000 at Jamaica; At Sunrise, $5,500 at Tropical; Overland, $4,500 at Garden State, and $5,500 at Tropical. Ariosa II had been raced at from $5,000 to $10,500 and won none of them.

In view of his win at $7,500, Rockport would seem to enjoy a Claiming Class edge over both Simmi J. and Yeoni. *But*—Yeoni outraced Rockport in their last, and while he's picking up four pounds under the conditions, Rockport is burdened with an extra twelve pounds. Simmi J. is obviously not at peak form. So Yeoni gets the nod.

While I have made an example of only one race, it was not chosen deliberately but at random and is, I feel, representative of the sort of confusion the new fan encounters in practically every race, whether he is wholly conscious of it or not.

The Class of Allowance races become even more confusing to the newer fan as soon as he discovers they embrace every grade of runner from the lowly maiden to the topnotch stakes performers without even the doubtful benefit of a juggled claiming tag to hint at his quality, or lack of it. The size of the purse controls the quality to some extent, for the classier runners are naturally going after the bigger pots of gold. Thus a grading of races by purses and a grading of tracks by purse distribution can be useful. We'll go into that in more detail later.

For now what we need to understand is that an allowance race at a cheaper track such as Charles Town, River Downs or Sunshine Park bears no quality relationship whatsoever to an allowance race run off at one of the top-grade tracks.

Nor is a $2500 claimer, for instance, at one of the cheaper tracks, the same quality as a $2500 claimer at one of the top tracks. They're both designated as $2500 claimers, or they're both designated as allowances, but there the resemblance ends. As a matter of fact, a handicap star at one of the cheap tracks could not compete successfully with the $2500 claimers of the most illustrious ovals.

When the fan accepts a classification from a cheap track as being equal to a similar call-out at one of the wealthy strips, he is doing himself a very serious disservice. This is perhaps one of the worst mistakes in connection with class the inexperienced player makes. But cheer up, we wouldn't make a disheartening statement like that if we didn't have the answer to the dilemma.

We hear at almost every turn around the tracks that "class will tell." Properly handled, this is doubtless true. But the thing that too few would-be selectors understand is that the so-called class of any horse is not a constant thing but varies with the sharpness of his condition, the distance of the contest under scrutiny, and the condition of the track.

Some horses "step way up" on an "off" track, or fall way below their fast track level as the case may be. Some horses rate a higher class figure at the route distances, or one certain route distance, than they do at a sprint distance. The opposite is true of certain other horses. And an otherwise competent performer, if he is off form, cannot outrun a fat lady, hence, regardless of how classy he might be while at peak form, his class is very close to zero when he is out of condition.

There is one other theory about class which is prevelant enough so that we should give it some space. The pace-handicapper will tell us that a classy but slow horse will beat a cheap fast horse because the classy one will run some one quarter of the race so fast as to run the cheapie into the ground. This is, of course, pure unadulterated hogwash.

In the first place, a slow horse is not a classy horse, and a really fast horse is not a cheap one. The mere fact that he is fast gives him claim to class, for speed and class are complementary and inseparable.

In the second place, if the so-called slow-class horse were actually able to turn on the heat for a quarter, why would the other horse necessarily follow close to the pace unless the jockey were soft in the head? And if the jockey ran his horse into the ground hanging onto a too-fast pace, why isn't this jockey error rather than a reflection on his mount's quality? It is bordering on the ridiculous to presume that a horse that consistently runs the six furlongs in, say, 1:10, can be beaten by a horse that runs the same distance in 1:12 if the race is truly run. The slower horse will need more than one fast quarter to turn back the speed merchant. He will need all the breaks in his favor, and the speed burner will have to run into a blind switch besides.

The more responsible pace-handicappers, while insisting that a class horse is one that has shown one quarter faster than his competition, will also expect his class selection to be capable of comparable overall speed for the full distance. This comes close to making sense, but if both horses have comparable overall speed for the distance, then there are simpler and better ways of delineating class than the tedious work of breaking races down into quarters.

Class is speed, and the courage and ability to sustain it over the distance of ground called-out in the conditions for today's race. It is the ability to handle the impost assigned, and do it better than the other contestants in a given field. Since all thoroughbreds can't be champions, and therefore top quality, they have to be re-evaluated in each race with respect to the quality and abilities of their competitors, and with respect to the distance of the race and the condition of the track.

Class is something else, at least from the viewpoint of the speculator. It is the ability to earn money, for if a horse does not make money for his owner, we can hardly expect him to make money for us, the speculators.

So let's investigate earn-ability as a basis for true class delineation.

4. Earn-Ability

Our monetary method of class delineation is based on earn-ability—per-race earn-ability, that is. To simply settle on the horse with the largest gross earnings would be wrong, for some pretty cheap horses manage to amass a respectable bundle. They race often and collect a little at a time, amassing a comfortable fortune over a period of, say, thirty or forty races. Another horse with an equal amount of gross earnings may have gotten his in three or four trips to the post. Obviously then, these two are not of the same class, since it is plain horse sense that the better horses are going to be sent after the bigger purses.

To pin this down, let's say each of these horses has won a gross of $16,000, horse A in forty races and horse B in four races. Horse A's earn-ability is $400. We get this by dividing the number of starts into the total amount of money earned during the period of these starts. In this same way we find that horse B's earn-ability is $4,000 per race. His class is 10/1 over horse A's.

In the *Form*, which is the racing paper most readily available to fans in all parts of the country, the money-earned "box" is in the upper right-hand corner of each horse's past performances. For those not familiar with it, it looks like this:

| 1957 | 5 2 2 0 | $12,450 |
| 1956 | 15 4 3 0 | $19,450 |

From this particular "box score" it can be readily seen that this horse has improved in class considerably in 1957 over 1956. This is not particularly surprising since he was a three-year-old in 1956 and has now attained his growth and strength as well as some invaluable racing experience.

By dividing the number of starts in each case into the gross earnings for that year it is seen that this one was a $1,300 horse in 1956, and is a $2,500 horse so far in 1957. Or, by combining both years, the number of starts would be twenty, and the total earnings, and the average per-race earn-ability roughly $1600. Perhaps a truer picture is obtained if we combine the two years for our average, provided the two years comprise the current year and last year. Frequently, we will find the "box score" made up of last year's record and the previous year, in which case we would use only last year, assuming that the previous year is too far back to be of value in the present.

On the other hand, it can be argued that using only the current year gives a more up-to-date evaluation of present class. (You will remember we mentioned the fact that class is not necessarily a constant but will vary from time to time.) However, in the early months of a new year, it will be found that many of the horses have been unraced in the current year or have been raced only a very few times. Consequently there is hardly enough data to go on. If the fan wants to use only the current year, he should make sure each horse has raced a minimum of three times. If there are any in the group which have not, then by all means use the current year and last year combined.

The newer fan probably feels all this long division comes

under the heading of a good deal of tedious work, and this would doubtless be so if we had to work it out to the exact dollar, but we do not. To take the pain and tedium out of this chore, an inexpensive slide rule will give sufficient accuracy. And anyone can learn to do multiplication and/or division on a slide rule in a matter of minutes. And once he has become adept through practice, he can determine the earn-ability of each horse in a given contest in five or ten minutes. A mighty small investment in time in return for which we will know exactly where the Class contention is in the race we're studying.

While it was never intended that this should develop into a one-factor system, still the strength of this thing is rather amazing when asked to stand up alone. To demonstrate the power behind this earn-ability-class, I have run off a thirty-day workout at Sunshine Park for the month of February, 1956, using absolutely nothing else to augment it. In each race, I have accepted as the selection, the horse showing the highest earn-ability figure, even though, as was the case in a number of instances, there might only be a one-dollar difference between first and second choice. And I have taken a selection for each and every race run during the month, from the lowly maidens through the feature events, and from the shortest sprints to the longest routes, and without regard to the changes in track conditions.

In short, I have given this the acid test, and the results obtained more than justify my claims for the method of determining class. Certainly, quality, arrived at in this way, would seem to substantiate the bromide that "class will tell."

This workout comprises 225 selections, one for each and every race run at Sunshine Park during February of 1956. 68 of them won at an average mutuel of $8.05. This is 30% winners, yielding a net profit of 21.7% on total invested capital. This win percentage is comparable to the national

WORKOUT

DATE	RACE	HORSE	WIN	PLACE	SHOW
2/1	1	Platterette	$ . . .	$ 4.00	$ 2.90
	2	Bob O Boy	7.90	4.00	2.80
	3	Juke	. . .	26.60	14.00
	4	Jimmy's First	4.60	2.80	2.60
	5	Hit Back	. . .	3.60	2.70
	6	Just Barbara	8.20	3.80	3.00
	7	Cant O'Mar	4.80	3.20	3.00
	8	A Gem	18.40	4.40	3.40
	9	Bridge Watch	3.70	2.70	2.20
2/2	1	Firey One	. . .	. . .	. . .
	2	Shaker Lee	5.10	3.70	3.10
	3	Oalo	. . .	8.20	5.30
	4	Chance Tip	. . .	. . .	. . .
	5	Petite Lassie	6.50	3.70	3.00
	6	Not Bad	. . .	. . .	2.60
	7	Whistle's Bro.	$ . . .	$ . . .	$ . . .
	8	Sheriff Bracey	10.50	5.10	2.70
	9	Put Out	3.90	3.00	2.30
2/3	1	Bean Beau	. . .	. . .	3.20
	2	Magic Choice	5.40	4.30	4.00
	3	Miss Allright	. . .	11.00	6.20
	4	Dolphie	. . .	. . .	. . .
	5	Mackey's Boy	26.30	6.70	4.00
	6	London	. . .	. . .	. . .
	7	Hap Glaudi	4.80	3.80	2.80
	8	Thee And Me	4.30	2.90	2.60
	9	Reveille	4.10	3.10	2.70
2/4	1	Clouded Sun	. . .	. . .	3.10
	2	Jerky	7.10	4.00	3.30
	3	Charlie's Brook	4.30	3.50	2.50
	4	Miss Minstrel	. . .	3.40	2.60
	5	Elevenpoint	. . .	. . .	2.70
	6	Imurguy	. . .	. . .	. . .
	7	Rock Pilot	5.40	4.00	3.50
	8	Calm Warrior	. . .	. . .	. . .

DATE	RACE	HORSE	WIN	PLACE	SHOW
	9	Busy Evening	. . .	3.80	2.80
2/6	1	Greek Dancer	. . .	. . .	. . .
	2	Destino's Date	. . .	. . .	. . .
	3	Halara	11.90	5.90	4.90
	4	Skyolater	$20.10	$ 7.00	$ 3.80
	5	Aviette	. . .	. . .	. . .
	6	Jean's Pride	6.90	4.80	3.90
	7	Ziggity	. . .	3.20	3.00
	8	Night Baker	. . .	6.30	4.30
	9	Charity Ball	3.50	2.70	2.20
2/7	1	Jean The Joker	. . .	. . .	. . .
	2	So Easy	. . .	. . .	. . .
	3	Idle Boy	. . .	. . .	. . .
	4	Blue Whiz Kid	. . .	. . .	. . .
	5	Aaron F.	14.00	7.30	4.90
	6	Tint Straw	. . .	. . .	. . .
	7	Cant O'Mar	5.40	3.30	2.60
	8	Shiny Knight	. . .	3.10	2.40
	9	Hyopolis	. . .	. . .	2.80
2/8	1	Bad News	4.10	3.00	2.40
	2	Dark Signorina	. . .	. . .	. . .
	3	Reine Lea	. . .	. . .	. . .
	4	Devil's Sound	15.50	8.40	5.30
	5	Hit Back	4.80	3.30	2.80
	6	Voyante	. . .	. . .	. . .
	7	Brassy Miss	. . .	3.50	2.50
	8	Bob O Boy	4.00	3.00	2.50
	9	Sammy S.	. . .	. . .	. . .
2/9	1	Coonamasset	$ . . .	$ . . .	$ . . .
	2	Hypostyle	. . .	. . .	2.40
	3	Brother G.	. . .	3.50	3.30
	4	Hoop Gano	. . .	. . .	2.30
	5	Attention Mark	. . .	3.60	3.10
	6	Pryner	4.80	3.60	2.80
	7	London	. . .	12.20	3.90
	8	Reveille	. . .	4.70	3.40
	9	Bramble Son	5.60	3.30	2.80
2/10	1	Clouded Sun	. . .	5.10	3.30

DATE	RACE	HORSE	WIN	PLACE	SHOW
	2	Chance Tip	6.40	3.60	3.70
	3	Marsh Hen	3.70	2.80	2.30
	4	Song Stylist	. . .	. . .	2.50
	5	Steak Bone	5.50	3.50	2.30
	6	Whistle's Bro.	. . .	. . .	. . .
	7	Luscious Fruit	. . .	. . .	. . .
	8	Lady Elect	. . .	. . .	. . .
	9	Son Joss	9.00	3.80	3.40
2/11	1	Val-O-Val	. . .	. . .	. . .
	2	Almenow	. . .	. . .	7.10
	3	No Harvest	4.60	3.00	2.90
	4	Henry D.M.	20.70	8.30	4.60
	5	Propeller			
	6	Night Baker	$ . . .	$ . . .	$ . . .
	7	Deep Thought	7.00	3.30	3.30
	8	Fleet Factor	. . .	. . .	5.00
	9	Time For Fun	. . .	. . .	. . .
2/13	1	Platterette	. . .	4.40	2.90
	2	Myrna Arlene	. . .	. . .	. . .
	3	Reine Lea	. . .	3.30	2.80
	4	Brother G.	3.30	2.90	2.40
	5	Magic Choice	. . .	. . .	. . .
	6	Reserve Fund	. . .	4.30	4.10
	7	Jane E.	. . .	. . .	13.80
	8	Joyce Gober	. . .	4.00	3.50
	9	What A Peach	. . .	. . .	. . .
2/14	1	Ala Carte	. . .	. . .	. . .
	2	*Crystal Vision f	. . .	18.20	5.80
	3	Tourney	. . .	. . .	. . .
	4	Dark Signorina	. . .	. . .	. . .
	5	Hoop Gano	. . .	. . .	. . .
	6	Little Brother	7.60	3.90	3.50
	7	Steppin' Pappy	. . .	2.80	2.50
	8	*Voyante	. . .	. . .	2.80
	9	Wellfleet	. . .	. . .	5.50
2/15	1	Clouded Sun	9.70	3.70	3.80
	2	Dandy John	. . .	. . .	. . .
	3	Coast Home	$ . . .	$ . . .	$ . . .

DATE	RACE	HORSE	WIN	PLACE	SHOW
	4	Broken Bow	. . .	. . .	12.70
	5	Reveillé	. . .	3.50	2.80
	6	Ziggity	4.70	2.90	2.60
	7	Rock Dozer	. . .	. . .	. . .
	8	Hit Back	. . .	2.70	2.50
	9	Night Baker	. . .	. . .	. . .
2/16	1	Destino's Date	. . .	. . .	. . .
	2	Wellfleet	. . .	. . .	5.10
	3	Almeda Acres	4.60	3.30	2.70
	4	Sun-One	. . .	. . .	. . .
	5	Very Stylish	. . .	. . .	. . .
	6	Bobby's Bull	. . .	. . .	2.80
	7	Cant O'Mar	. . .	. . .	. . .
	8	Calm Warrior	10.80	4.40	3.30
	9	Attention Mark	. . .	3.00	2.50
2/17	1	Secret Passion	. . .	. . .	3.20
	2	Idle Boy	. . .	9.10	5.30
	3	Miss Phelia	. . .	. . .	. . .
	4	Alladier	. . .	. . .	. . .
	5	Sad Zac	. . .	. . .	. . .
	6	Bell Diver	6.80	3.70	3.20
	7	Brassy Miss	. . .	. . .	. . .
	8	Mystic Gold	. . .	. . .	. . .
	9	Count Pur	. . .	9.40	4.20
2/18	1	Mr. Pan	$ . . .	$ . . .	$ . . .
	2	Myrna Arlene	26.20	10.80	7.70
	3	Ann-Mar	. . .	. . .	. . .
	4	I Froo	. . .	. . .	4.20
	5	Bob O Boy	. . .	. . .	3.70
	6	Tint Straw	. . .	. . .	. . .
	7	Put Out	. . .	. . .	. . .
	8	Night Baker	14.30	7.50	5.80
	9	O'Reigh	. . .	. . .	. . .
2/20	1	Cherry Stone	. . .	4.90	3.90
	2	Platterette	. . .	2.70	2.20
	3	Joe's Jeep	. . .	8.10	4.60
	4	Game Winnie	. . .	3.00	2.30
	5	Hoop Gano	. . .	. . .	. . .

DATE	RACE	HORSE	WIN	PLACE	SHOW
	6	Sad Zac	7.00	4.00	3.00
	7	Hit Back	3.70	2.70	2.10
	8	Flicker Light	. . .	. . .	. . .
	9	Mystic Gold	4.90	2.90	2.80
2/21	1	Coast Home	. . .	6.20	5.90
	2	Challcote	. . .	. . .	. . .
	3	Plain Jim	. . .	. . .	. . .
	4	Hypostyle	. . .	. . .	. . .
	5	Cash Request	. . .	. . .	. . .
	6	Clouded Sun	. . .	. . .	4.00
	7	Sunday Favor	$ . . .	$ . . .	$ . . .
	8	Red Petticoat	. . .	. . .	. . .
	9	Just A Foot	. . .	. . .	2.90
2/22	1	Miss Phelia	7.50	5.60	3.90
	2	Coral Princess	. . .	. . .	. . .
	3	Steak Bone	. . .	. . .	. . .
	4	Brassy Miss	. . .	11.10	5.00
	5	B. Prompt	. . .	. . .	. . .
	6	Thee And Me	3.90	3.10	2.60
	7	Daring Spirit	8.20	4.80	3.30
	8	Hiya-Sailor	. . .	. . .	. . .
	9	Busy Evening	6.80	3.30	2.30
2/23	1	Jubilee	. . .	2.70	2.40
	2	De Music	. . .	. . .	. . .
	3	Wellfleet	. . .	. . .	. . .
	4	Brownskin	. . .	2.80	2.20
	5	Sarah E.	. . .	. . .	3.00
	6	Almenow	. . .	. . .	. . .
	7	Marsh Hen	. . .	3.30	2.40
	8	Voyante	8.00	4.20	3.10
	9	Bad News	. . .	. . .	11.10
2/24	1	First Return	. . .	. . .	3.00
	2	Firey One	. . .	3.90	3.40
	3	Cute Storm	17.70	6.70	3.70
	4	Idle Boy	$ . . .	$ . . .	$ . . .
	5	Challcote	. . .	. . .	2.90
	6	Whistle's Bro.	7.00	3.00	2.50
	7	Rock Dozer	7.00	3.40	3.10

DATE	RACE	HORSE	WIN	PLACE	SHOW
	8	Joyce Gober	. . .	2.80	2.80
	9	Pipetime	. . .	. . .	2.60
2/25	1	Coonamasset	. . .	. . .	. . .
	2	Trenton Sand	. . .	. . .	6.90
	3	Ten Goal	. . .	. . .	5.90
	4	Reveille	5.40	3.70	2.80
	5	B. Prompt	. . .	. . .	5.40
	6	Cant O'Mar	. . .	4.90	4.20
	7	Rock Pilot	4.50	3.90	2.70
	8	Hit Back	. . .	. . .	. . .
	9	Flicker Light	. . .	3.90	3.80
2/27	1	Secret Passion	. . .	. . .	3.40
	2	Hypostyle	. . .	. . .	2.80
	3	Chance Tip	5.80	3.50	3.50
	4	Brentwoodian	. . .	. . .	. . .
	5	Pennfleur	. . .	3.40	2.60
	6	Hoop Gano	. . .	. . .	. . .
	7	Devil's Sound	. . .	. . .	. . .
	8	Andromeda	14.80	7.30	3.90
	9	Platterette	6.50	3.70	2.80
2/28	1	Third Point	$ . . .	$ . . .	$ . . .
	2	Destino's Date	. . .	. . .	. . .
	3	Jubilee	. . .	. . .	2.30
	4	Long Lake	. . .	11.20	5.60
	5	Magic Choice	6.80	4.20	3.10
	6	Mab	. . .	. . .	. . .
	7	Herb S.	13.70	5.90	3.70
	8	Propeller	. . .	4.90	4.20
	9	Idle Boy	. . .	. . .	3.10
2/29	1	Range Cardinal	. . .	. . .	. . .
	2	Attention Mark	4.20	3.20	2.50
	3	Old Booty	. . .	. . .	3.90
	4	B. Prompt	. . .	. . .	2.40
	5	Mr. Willmes	. . .	. . .	2.20
	6	Hit Back	. . .	. . .	. . .
	7	Ace Reporter	9.50	5.00	4.30
	8	Bramble Sun	7.20	4.00	3.50
	9	Fred B.	6.60	4.40	3.00

average for bet favorites. But the average mutuel for bet favorites is too low to yield a profit.

The place and show breakdowns on this workout are interesting, too. Of the 225 selections, 111 ran either first or second (49%) and the yield on total invested capital was 19%. (Average mutuel, $4.85.)

For the show, 147 of these selections finished in-the-money (65%). The yield for show, like the place, was 19%. (Average show mutuel, $4.40.)

Asterisk (*) indicates that either the stablemate, in the case of a stable entry, or a horse coupled in a mutuel field, accounted for the placing.

Considering the burden we placed on our earn-ability-class method, this workout is remarkable. It definitely establishes the solidity of this approach. And though it was not conceived as a system but as a basic approach to the class problem, still the results indicate that it could be played profitably without further embellishment. On the basis of $20 flat wagers, the win action would have produced a net profit of $976.00 for the short month. From $20 flat place play, a net profit of $885.00; and from show, $875.00. And a very insignificant couple of hundred dollars operating capital would have been more than adequate to keep the thing solvent at all times.

Actually, no single factor should be forced to assume the burden of producing consistently successful selections, but it is nonetheless gratifying to know we have a class angle that *will* stand up by itself. Especially as a show method, this leaves little to be desired if one does not wish to become too involved. Cashing 65% of his bets for a 19% yield on total invested capital is a goal many professional speculators never achieve. Some of them are quite content to earn 3%, and be not deceived, it is possible to amass a comfortable fortune on 3% yield because of the very rapid turn-over and re-employment of one's operating capital.

Perhaps the greatest boon we have gained through the earn-ability-class method is that we no longer need sweat over claiming tags, and we no longer have to become involved in long and tedious horse-by-horse analysis to locate the class in an allowance race, for now we can put a cash value on class, whether the beetle be a maiden, a claimer, an allowance competitor, or shows up most frequently in the handicap grades. In each of these divisions there are grades within grades, but earn-ability trots them all out in the light to be viewed and considered, or summarily discarded.

Earn-ability is the new look at class and will save the budding selector much time and uncertainty.

We'll see this in practical application in later chapters as we develop various systems and handicapping procedures.

5. Speed-Ability

While class can be said to be the *basic* selection medium, *speed* is the utility factor. Properly used, it can either validate or invalidate the basic class. It can be used to determine the present physical condition of a horse, and it can be used as one means of establishing his consistency. Since we know speed to be useful in so many ways, we can only conclude that the fans who have bad luck with it are not employing it properly.

The rabid class advocates are inclined to sneer at the proponents of speed, and vice-versa. Each is wrong. Speed and class make a powerful team when allowed to properly complement each other.

There just isn't any arguing with the truism that the fastest horse *should* get home free, the fact that he does not always do so notwithstanding. In a hoss race, with a field of plunging thoroughbreds crowding and vying for position, traffic problems are created which sometimes make our best analytical figures look silly. Class horses, speed burners, and gems of consistency alike are victims of bad breaks on occasion.

Nobody wins them all, no matter how astute a selector he may be. But the fan who learns how to use each factor to its best advantage will automatically maintain sufficiently high averages to guarantee consistent profits.

So we're going to study speed, its uses and misuses, with the idea of making it work hand-in-glove with the other factors. And perhaps the best way to learn its best uses is to understand its abuses.

Let's start with the speed ratings found in both the *Form* and the *Telegraph*. These are based on the track record at the oval where the rating is earned. The record, in all cases, is given a value, a par or norm, of 100. A horse setting a new track record is given a rating of 100 plus one more point for each fifth of a second (each length) by which he lowers the record. Thus if he lowers the record by two fifths, his rating for this race is 102. If he had turned in an elapsed time two-fifths slower than the track record, his rating would have been 98.

This is probably the best ready-made rating system there is, and it is admittedly a strong temptation to accept it and use it rather than go to the additional work of developing a superior rating system. But the truth of the matter is, the speed ratings furnished us by the *Form* and the *Telegraph*, except in very special cases, are not trustworthy. Thus the fan who sneers at speed because he has had haphazard results from the use of these speed ratings, has not given the speed factor a fair trial, and is denying himself the benefits to be gained from the proper use of this power-packed factor.

Let's see why we shouldn't rely too heavily on these ready-made speed ratings. In the first place, these ratings are not comparable, one distance to another. By this we mean, we cannot take a six-furlong rating and presume this gives us a line on what the horse will do at a mile and an eighth, or a mile, or seven furlongs. And of course, the fast track speed ratings are not comparable, even with a like distance, with "off" track ratings. Five-and-a-half-furlong ratings are too fast by far to be acceptable as evidence of what the same horse will do at six furlongs. And so on through the list.

What is the special set of circumstances when these ratings are trustworthy? When all entrants in the race have raced recently, at this track, at this distance, and under fast track conditions, and provided the track record hasn't been broken during these recent races. For if the record has just been lowered by two-fifths, the speed ratings of all contestants except the new record-holder will suddenly become ⅖ths of a second slower than they were a few days before with exactly the same effort.

This, then, points up the real weakness of the speed ratings, the fact that they are based on the records at each track of the distances customarily carded. Thus while Swaps hung up world's and track records seemingly everywhere he went, thus making the ratings for those distances at those tracks unusually slow, the cheap tracks that are never graced by a visit from such super-speed horses as Swaps and company, and consequently have much slower records upon which to base the par value from which ratings are figured, are quite likely to produce fabulously high speed ratings for comparatively slow elapsed times. Thus if we accept speed ratings from these divergent areas, assuming they were to meet at, say, a winter meeting (and believe me, they do) we would find ourselves backing the cheapie which hasn't a chance of matching strides with the seemingly slower horse that has been forced to earn his speed rating after Swaps has preceded him.

This is an exaggeration, of course, but one that is justified to bring home a very important point. To bring it, now, into proper focus, let's consider a winter track like Sunshine Park. Horses come here from all over the Middle West, East, Northeast, and Canada, bringing with them speed ratings made from a fine assortment of track records. For instance, here are the tracks represented in only the first race of the second day of the meeting: Wod, F.E., Was., A.P., Crn, C.D., Beu, Ran, EIP, Fgs, F.M., Whe, Cka, Suf, Rkm, Nar, L.D., S.P. (preceding year), H.P., H.O., Wdb, F.P., Det, and Wat. (Jan. 26, 1957)

Enough to give you the shudders, isn't it? But hear this. How would you like to back a 90 rating, fresh from Crn for 6 furlongs run on a fast strip in 1:14⅘, instead of an 88 made at A.P. for 6 furlongs in 1:11⅕?

Do you begin to get the idea of the kind of thing you can let yourself in for if you follow speed ratings blindly? Is it any wonder some fans sneer at speed?

What, then, are we going to do about speed?

We're going to make our own ratings, comparable for the various distance and varying stages of "off" track, using as par the twelve-second furlong (fast track) accepted by horsemen everywhere as standard. This we will use on all sprint distances with the track in a dry condition. This will increase gradually through the various "off" stages until we are using 12⅘ second furlongs for the sprint distances in the heavy going. Similar adjustments are allowed for increasing distance and the various "off" stages for route races until we reach 13⅗ second furlongs which will be used for rating 1¼ miles in the heavy footing.

In the interest of saving the student-fan time and unnecessary work, we have prepared charts giving the standards for the various distances and track conditions. For instance, if it is six furlongs, fast track, that is needed, the chart for sprints tells us the standard is 1:12 (6 x 12 equals 72 seconds which equals one minute 12 seconds).

If the nag we are investigating ran the six panels two-fifths faster than this, and using the standard as zero in all cases, he gets a rating of minus 2 (-2). If his race was two fifths slower, his rating becomes plus 2 ($+2$). A minus figure, then, will always be recognized as faster than a plus figure.

SPRINT DISTANCE STANDARDS

Track Cond.	5 F.	5½ F.	6 F.	6½ F.	7 F.
Fast	1:00	1:06	1:12	1:18	1:24
Good-Sloppy	1:01	1:07	1:13⅕	1:19⅕	1:25⅗
Slow	1:02	1:08	1:14⅖	1:20⅖	1:27⅕
Muddy	1:03	1:09⅖	1:15⅗	1:21⅘	1:28⅘
Heavy	1:04	1:10⅖	1:16⅘	1:23⅕	1:30⅖

ROUTE DISTANCE STANDARDS

Track Cond.	Mile	1¹⁄₁₆	1⅛	1¼	1½
Fast	1:37⅗	1:45⅗	1:53⅖	2:05	2:31
Good-Sloppy	1:39⅖	1:47⅕	1:55⅕	2:08⅕	2:34⅕
Slow	1:40⅘	1:48⅘	1:57	2:10	2:36
Muddy	1:42	1:50⅗	1:58⅗	2:11⅗	2:37⅗
Heavy	1:44	1:51⅗	2:01⅗	2:14⅕	2:40⅕

We can now compare any or all distances and variety of "off" track with some degree of confidence. Confidence grows with usage. For the "in-between" distances: Add 4⅖ seconds to the mile standard for 1-70; 1³⁄₁₆ would be the halfway point between 1⅛ and 1¼; 1⅜, half the difference between 1¼ and 1½ for the track condition indicated.

The twelve-second furlong standard can also be used to advantage in rating workouts as in the case of a first-time starter: (2F., :24; 3F., :36; 4F., :48; 4½ F., :54), or one unraced recently but working too well to ignore.

The advantages of being able to assign a rating from the most recent race in the contestant's past performances should be self evident. Too often, when we have to go far back to find a race at today's distance and/or today's track condition we run the risk of rating the horse off of a peak condition effort, the fine sharp edge of which he has probably lost since. Or we run an equal risk of rating from a race back when he was off form, and thus miss something good if he is now at peak.

Rating him off of a recent race regardless of distance or

condition of the track allows us to draw our analytical comparison of all contestants as they are now, not as they were two, three or six months ago.

Let's run through some examples so the newer fans among us will be sure to understand our working methods. Let's use our charts first on the country cousins we made an example of. The good horse from A.P. that had earned only an 88 because of the relatively high track record at A.P. for the distance, now becomes a minus four (−4), while the horrible hide from Crn that was hiding behind a 90 because of the comparatively slow track record at that track, now assumes his correct speed level with our rating of a plus fourteen (+14).

Let's pick a *Form* at random. It's March 11, 1957, "Blue Monday" at Gulfstream Park where the track is fast. The first race is carded at six furlongs, and the conditions call out three-year-olds and a claiming price of $6,250. Not that the conditions will influence us in this instance since we are only going to test some ratings, but we should form the habit of always reading the conditions and understanding them.

A lady horse by the name of Tillie Temple gets the fastest rating. She won a six-furlong waltz at Hialeah on March 1 when the track was heavy. She negotiated the trip in 1:15⅘. Our standard for a heavy six panels is 1:16⅘, so we assign Tillie Temple a −5. Next in line is Kensington. This gelding ran second to Tillie in that heavy track race, and finished two lengths behind her. His time therefore was 1:16¼ and his rating, −3. Next in line is the colt Revolark. His last race was on March 2nd, at six furlongs over a fast strip. He was beaten 6¼ lengths by a speedster who did the job in 1:10⅖. Since our standard for 6 F. on a fast track is 1:12, the winner's rating was −8. But Revolark's time was 6¼ lengths slower, so his rating is −1¾.

Since the track is fast today at G.P., we want to see some evidence of Tillie's fast-strip-ability.

Her previous race was on the fast, and at 6 F. at Detroit, but was so dull (a plus 12) that we suspect it may not be a true indication of her fast-track-ability. So we go on back until we find her best one. Off of this one, we assign her a plus one (+1) rating, a difference of six lengths from her recent heavy track race.

Kensington, also rated off of the heavy, likes the fast tracks even less. He sprints on the fast to ratings of 9, 9½, and worse.

Revolark with his −1¾, on the fast, is the indicated speed horse on today's kind of footing. He was returned the winner, while the other two again displayed their lack of enthusiasm for fast track racing by finishing down the track.

In the second race, the conditions were identical to those for the first. There are two contestants with minus ratings, all the rest having plus ratings, hence automatically dropped from consideration as not indicating peak condition, or sufficient ability to be a challenge to the top two.

On Her Way receives a −9 from a mud race at Hialeah, the distance the same as today's. This race was won in 1:13 flat, but On Her Way finished second, beaten four lengths. Our chart shows the mud standard for 6 F. to be 1:15⅗, so the filly's 1:13⅘ is nine points faster, hence −9.

Free And Busy raced last at Hialeah on March 1, 1957, and the track was heavy, the distance six furlongs. He won this and negotiated the distance in 1:15⅘. Our standard for a heavy 6 F. is 1:16⅘, so Free And Busy gets a rating of −5.

Since we had to rate both of these off of "off" track efforts, our next move is to see if either or both can run on a dry track.

On Her Way's previous race was on the fast at Tropical. She ran third, beaten 2½ lengths by the 1:11⅘ winner. This makes On Her Way 2½ points slower than the winner's −1, for a rating of plus 1½.

The previous race for Free And Busy was at Hialeah at today's distance and on a fast strip. He ran second to a 1:11⅘ winner, beaten 4½ lengths. Thus his rating is a plus 3½.

Since On Her Way has superior ratings in both the "off" and the fast, we can play her with confidence since the next fastest for a fast track is a plus 3 for Timely.

On Her Way, though off to a bad start, had little trouble turning back this field, taking down the front end of the purse by 1¼ lengths.

For some unaccountable reason, the dear wagering public established a hide by the name of Duke's Sandal as the bet favorite. One can only assume that this was the result of a whispering campaign, the spreading of a rumor that Duke's Sandal would be dusted off in this spot. There seems no other explanation, for the Duke had only about a quarter of the class of On Her Way by our earn-ability process, and a plus 12 as against On Her Way's −9. To make his popularity the more bewildering, he was beaten twenty-one lengths in his last race, at 6 F. on a fast track, and twenty-three lengths in his previous race at 1¹⁄₁₆. His only win shown in his past performances was at Tdn, which is hardly in the same league with G.P. (This will become evident when we touch on track grading in a later chapter.)

So the wagering public was so busy making Duke's Sandal an utterly false favorite that On Her Way was allowed to get on her way at a nice 9/2, paying $11.70 in the Mutuels. Free And Busy finished second.

In this there is a good, sound lesson. Never let the tote board alter your decision once your analysis or your system has pointed up a selection. I have collected as high as $124.00 for two by refusing to let the tote board stampede me into a blind switch.

Now let's look at the 7th, the Iron Mask Handicap **in**

which the racing secretary assigned the weights. The high weight went to Needles (126), a very handy young gentleman, especially noted for his sensational stretch drives. Second in the weight department is Admiral Vee with 119 pounds.

This Handicap was carded at 6½ furlongs. Nan's Mink gets a −11 off of a 6 F. effort at Hialeah on March 2. The track was fast. Admiral Vee gets a −10, earned in a stake race (HcpS) at New Orleans. This was at 1⅛ miles and the Admiral, a five-year-old horse, was shipped from Hialeah for that one race, then brought right back to compete at Gulfstream. The gamble did not pay off and, though beaten, Admiral Vee did make a reasonably fast trip around the F.G. oval.

Needles, rated off of a tc (turf course) waltz at 1³⁄₁₆ miles, at which time the turf course was designated as soft (sf), gets a −9¼. (We used the standard for a good track as being comparable to (sf).

These are the three highest ratings. Since none of them had raced at 6½ F. before, but all three had been out at 7 F., it might be helpful to compare them at this common distance to see if anything interesting evolves. As a result Nan's Mink got a plus 5; Admiral Vee got a −1½; and Needles got a −1. And believe it or not, that's the way they finished. Admiral Vee beat Needles by a nose, and Nan's Mink saved the show spot for himself.

Before we leave Gulfstream Park to check an "off" track at Sunshine Park, it is of passing interest to note that the race won by Revolark (the first at G.P.) was one of those special cases we mentioned where the *Form*'s speed ratings were quite reliable. All horses had recent fast track *Racing Form* speed ratings at today's distance at Hialeah which is the same (Florida) winter circuit with Gulfstream Park and immediately precedes it. Of these fast track R.F. speed ratings, Revolark's was the highest.

Now, let's see what happens to our rating system when it is required to select for an "off" track. Here is a muddy track at S.P. The date is February 4, 1956, and the race is a six-furlong claimer for four-year-olds and upward.

The three fastest ratings all came from 5½ F. fast track efforts. They were, Clouded Sun, 3½; Mardee C., 4¾; and Lady Cowboy, 9¼. In hunting for the best mudder among these three, we get a —3 for Mardee C., for a Heavy 6 F. effort; a plus 5 for Lady Cowboy for a 6 F. mud race at Nar; and a plus 11 for Clouded Sun from a sloppy five furlongs at L.D. This, of course, points the finger at Mardee C.

She won it by 7½ lengths without working up a sweat. Lady Cowboy was second and Clouded Sun third.

These examples should give the student-fan a working idea of how to proceed, keeping in mind that the speed factor, no more than the earn-ability-class factor, should be asked to stand alone. But the two factors used together, either in a handicap-analysis or in a system, can be a very gratifying experience in our feud with the racing secretary. While he concentrates on weight, we'll concentrate on speed and class and such other contributing factors as may be pertinent with a given set of circumstances.

Now that we have some facility in handling both earn-ability-class, and speed, it is time we give some thought to validating each through the study of the *condition*, or *form* factor.

6. Form Factor

We have already observed that if a horse is not in *condition*, or peak *form*, that he is virtually without class or speed. Any speed or class he may lay claim to by virtue of past performances is rendered ineffectual because he is not now physically able to reaffirm them.

For this reason, present peak form is the one factor we cannot afford to be without. It is the one factor without which —that is to say without evidence of sharp form—all other factors and figures are worthless.

Our selection must have the physical sharpness to validate and verify the figures we have worked up for him or the work we have done is pure, unadulterated pounding of sand in the proverbial rat hole. If we leave the condition factor to chance, we are indulging in gambling of the rankest sort and are almost certain to get what we deserve—and I do mean right in the bankroll.

Since it is so vitally important, perhaps some of you are wondering why we didn't discuss it earlier instead of waiting until chapter six. Our reason, of course, was that we felt that the newer hands should understand our basic conception of class, and our somewhat different approach to the speed problem so as better to grasp the importance and application of the condition factor. And speed, especially, is going to play an important role in helping us establish condition, particularly in the many cases where there is no visual evidence of sharpness in the recent past performances.

To explain this, let's say a trainer is running his horse into condition, and that he is not particularly anxious to have it become obvious when the nag starts coming to hand. He wants to capitalize on his hard work by a substantial wager as well as the purse, and he naturally feels he is entitled to the very best price he can get. He is bringing his horse to hand as quietly and unobtrusively as possible by the simple expedient of running him over his head. Even as the horse approaches peak form, he still looks bad to the casual and uninitiated observer who is looking for the obvious signs of sharpness, such as finishing, last time, close up in-the-money.

You and I, because we know how to use speed to point up peak condition, will not be fooled by the trainers' attempts to hide his sleeper. The proper application of the speed factor will tell us, when nothing else will, that this race, now, today, should be the one in which the now-sharp horse will be asked the question. And it stands to reason that we're going to get a better price on a hide that is just coming to hand than we could hope for on a horse that has already displayed his form for all to see. All too frequently, once form is obvious it is already too late for us to collect a bet, for a recent winner may have extended himself so much in order to win that last one that he will be incapable of another winning effort for some time to come.

Don't worry about this. We're going to learn how to detect this kind, too, and here again the correct application of the speed factor will tip us off. As we told you, speed is the *utility* factor.

So let's get down to cases.

Because of the opportunity for a price, the improving horse makes a nice betting tool, especially one that has not tipped his condition all over the place by running close up. We can spot this kind by the use of speed, and usually, the ready-made speed ratings in the *Form* or *Telegraph* can give us our first clue. If these speed ratings show a gradual improvement, regardless of where the horse has been finishing, we have visible, though not obvious (to the average fan), evidence of an improving horse. Whether he has improved *enough* at this time is still for us to determine.

By gradual improvement, we mean over the last three or four races, if they have been run within, say, the past six weeks or so. Suppose the fourth race back produced a ready-made rating of 72; the third race back, a 75; the second one back, a 77, and the last one an 80. There can be little doubt this beastie is coming to hand. And if we can establish that that final 80 is not the equivalent of his *best* race, we have legitimate reason to expect further improvement in today's race.

To determine this, the *Form* is easier than the *Telegraph*, in that the *Form* supplies us with an index for each race. This index gives a list of all contestants, with the best time for each made either during the current year or last year. If the horse has not raced at this distance during this period, or if he was beaten more than seventeen lengths, he will not have an elapsed time listed. If he does not have a time listed, he is a doubtful quantity which could be ignored. On the other hand, it's possible to be beaten by this kind. However, if each and every contestant is represented by an elapsed time figure in the index, our work is routine.

If our improving hoss is getting close to, but has not yet equalled his best time as shown in the index, we can reasonably expect further improvement. If he still has a good way to go to equal his best time, then we can assume he is not yet ready to run back to his best. Sometimes a horse "wakes up" suddenly, but one such as the one showing gradual improvement in our example is apt to continue to improve slowly and steadily, unless he has already reached his full capability. If he has equalled his best time without winning, then the trainer may have missed the boat by not dropping him in class soon enough.

The ideal situation, of course, is the one where we find our nag just a point or two below his best in that last race, with anticipated improvement today, plus sufficient earnability-class and overall speed to cope with his competition.

He need not be the highest speed in the index if we are satisfied that any horse showing higher index speed is *not* at peak.

For the most part, the index times are given for a fast track, but occasionally, we will find a time for one or the other stages of "off" track, thus: 1:12⅘ sy. In a case like this we can employ our standards and our own rating system to determine if the nag is close to his best.

If we do not have the *Form*, but have the *Telegraph*, which supplies no index, we must make our comparison from the best race listed in the past performances keeping in mind that this is not necessarily the best race the horse may have been capable of during the longer period of time utilized by the index.

If the index time and the time for the contestant's last race are one and the same, that is, the horse, in his last race, has just established the index time shown, we should not expect him to do better again today. In fact, we have no reason to expect he will even do as well.

While it is a well-established fact that most horses can not be counted upon to repeat a winning performance, it is quite possible that he will do so if the win just recorded was ac-

complished in slower time than his best time. It could mean
that his trainer found a soft spot for him in which he was able
to win without overextending himself, and thus may have
plenty of edge left for another win—if properly placed, of
course.

To emphasize these various points, and clarify the procedure for the newer hands, a few examples will help.

The sixth race at G.P. on March 11, 1957 furnishes us
with some interesting situations. It is an allowance affair for
a purse of $4,000, for four-year-olds and upward. It is for
non-winners of $3,000 three times in 1956-57 with pounds
allowed off for failure to win stipulated amounts of money
within certain stipulated periods of time. Let it be sufficient
to say that it is a wide-open waltz from the standpoint of the
racing secretary's conditions. It is the sort of thing to make
a young man age before his time—a beetle race that could
doubtless not be conceived in any other than Horace Wade's
agile brain.

Nine horses accepted the conditions for this contest, which
is carded at 1$\frac{1}{16}$ miles, and all but Rockcastle show an
index time for the distance, and it is rare indeed that we see
a field so evenly matched from the standpoint of the index
best times.

Fresh Meadow shows the fastest time by $\frac{1}{5}$ of a second
with 1:43$\frac{1}{5}$; Sam Slick, Cedrus, Grand Canyon, Ratheram,
and Homeplace all have a best time of 1:43$\frac{2}{5}$; Old Roman
shows 1:43$\frac{3}{5}$; and Lead Scout, 1:43$\frac{4}{5}$.

We can eliminate Fresh Meadow at once, for just a quick
glance at his speed-line (speed rating column immediately
following the class-line in the *Form*) tells us that he is staling
off, for his past three races, all at Hialeah, show a steady
decline. His third race back earned a 91; his second race
back an 86; and his last race an 85. Without this evidence
of declining speed-ability, we might easily have been fooled

about his condition, for he ran a close-up second in his last race, the slowest of the three. This was due to some clever spotting by his trainer which is not repeated in this race, for we can give Fresh Meadow only a −3 off that last race. Today's field runs mostly to minus 16s, 17s, and 18s.

We have no choice but to conclude that the number one index horse has shot his bolt.

Let's examine the speed-lines for the others for a quick evaluation of their chances from a condition standpoint. Reading the speed-line from the third race back to the present, Sam Slick shows *88-96-84*. These three were all within a six-week period at Hialeah, the most recent one on March 4. Sam seems to have left his race on the track with that 96 effort.

Cedrus has only one recent race, a month before. It was his first outing since Pimlico in 1956 and the rest did' him some good for he ran faster at first asking at Hialeah (92) than for either of his last two wins at Pim. His speed-line looks like this: 84-79-*92*.

Old Roman, 97-86-69 (all at Hialeah)
Grand Canyon, 79-79-72 (all at Hia)
Ratheram, 95-49sl-85 (Trp & Hia)
Lead Scout, *88*-82-*90* (all at Hia)
Homeplace, *83*-81-*89* (all at Hia)
Fresh Meadow 91-86-85 (Hia)
Rockcastle—no Index—79-86-69gd. (Hia)

We have already definitely eliminated Rockcastle and Fresh Meadow, with Sam Slick being doubtful. We now drop Old Roman, Grand Canyon, and Ratheram for obvious reasons. Lead Scout, Homeplace and Cedrus are our three real contenders.

As we said in the beginning of this, the race is wide open, a real toughie, but we have got it boiled down to the three most logical contenders. They're all at, or very near, peak, and two of them, Cedrus and Homeplace, share the very fast index time of 1:43⅗ while Lead Scout's best time is ⅗ths slower. There would be little point in trying to prove anything further with speed, so if we must satisfy our curiosity as to which one would be the ultimate selection, we would try to break the tie on earn-ability-class.

On this, then, Cedrus has an average per-race earn-ability of $900; Homeplace, $850; and Lead Scout, who has all but been eliminated from consideration on index speed, $770 per-race earn-ability.

Cedrus has a slight advantage, then, on the class factor, though, frankly, a conservative speculator looking for a good spot play would pass this race.

Anyhow, it did make an interesting problem simply because it was so tough, and Cedrus did win it, though at a $5.40 mutuel he was underlaid.

Now let's reconsider a couple of races we looked at in the previous chapter. In the first race at G.P. on March 11, it will be recalled we isolated Tillie Temple, Kensington, and Revolark as our three contenders on the speed factor. Let us now see if our index method of determining condition or form strengthens or detracts from our previous decision (without the condition factor) that Revolark could be played.

Tillie Temple had a −5 off of a (hy) race at six furlongs, which she had won handily. But her best time à la index on a fast track was 1:12⅕ at Detroit, which is a plus 1. In going backward on Tillie's past performances we find her only other winning performance was also on an "off" track. She won by seven lengths in the mud at Detroit and earned a −1. So both of her "off" track ratings are superior to her dry track index time. This is something we file away in our memory for future use. Speed-line, 87-76gd-76-66hy.

Kensington was rated a −3, and a speed-line of 78-77-64hy. His 1:13 best time (index) earned at Tropical hardly recommends him, even though his −3 says he was sharp in that "off" track race.

Revolark earned his $-1\frac{3}{4}$ on a fast track at Hialeah at today's distance and, incidentally, set up his best time for the index in this race. Now we said earlier in this chapter that a horse whose best time was earned in his last race could not be expected to exceed this good time today, or even to equal it. Among the three-year-olds, this rule cannot be held inflexible. For we also reported that a three-year-old gains strength and stature during the first half to three-quarters of this formative year, until he has improved to the point where he can match strides with four-year-olds by September. So from this we have to admit that the sophomores not only *can,* but we *expect* them to, improve with racing. The rule will still hold in this one respect, however. If the youngster *won* that last one while setting up his best time, we'll consider him as having been used up for the present. But Revolark did not win, and did not appear to be pressed too hard since he finished third, six and a half lengths back of the winner. And Revolark has the fastest, best time, in the index, 1:11⅗ which he made while lugging 122 pounds. He is in with 115 pounds today, which is another reason to expect he might improve his index time. (Speed-line, 74-82-87.)

As a matter of fact, he did not, but he did turn in a good 1:11⅗, which was good enough to get the job done.

In the second race our two minus-rating horses were On Her Way and Free And Busy, remember? We will also recall On Her Way had substantially more earn-ability-class than either Duke's Sandal, the betting public's false favorite, or Free And Busy. So now let's see how the classy little lady stacks up on our condition wrinkle.

While we rated her off of a race in the mud, we find there is only one horse in the index with better dry track time, a beastie by the name of Buzzie. We can best see his decline by first looking at his *Racing Form* speed-line, then converting it to our own speed ratings to better evaluate that heavy track race of his. His R.F. speed-line was 91-78-38hy. Changing over to our ratings we get (-4)-$(7\frac{1}{4})$-(23). It can be seen from this that Buzzie has gone way back from his best race. He rates no further thought from us.

Now we must investigate Free And Busy, for he has the same index time as On Her Way. We see that he won his last race in the heavy going. This is against him, but his speed-line looks good when translated to our own version . . . $(4\frac{3}{4})$-$(3\frac{1}{2})$-(-5) . . . Comparing this to On Her Way's speed-line . . . $(7\frac{1}{4})$-$(1\frac{1}{2})$-(-9) . . . while both are good, that of On Her Way shows definite superiority. And that's the way it worked out. On Her Way beat Free And Busy by $1\frac{1}{4}$ lengths.

Incidentally, this was one of those races where the Index carried two best times with "off" track notations. Untimely, 1:15⅗m, and Surry, 1:17m. The first at Washington Park and the other at Churchill Downs. Reducing this to ratings we get a -1 for Untimely to compare with On Her Way's index of -2, leaving the Gangway filly still the choice. (Surry was scratched before post time.)

While we suggested the use of the ready-made speed ratings to determine, quickly, the improvement, or lack of it over the last several races, we think that despite the extra work, it is a good habit to form to not accept a situation until borne out by a check with our own ratings. This is, of course, practically a *must* where "off" track efforts are involved, and really should be considered so where different fast track distances are involved.

There were three races on this March 11 card at Gulfstream Park where the index could not be used to help us to determine condition. They were the 3rd, the 7th, and the 9th.

In the 3rd, only one of the entrants had been the distance, six and a half furlongs, and he was subsequently scratched. In the seventh, at the same distance, only three of the contestants had recorded index time. If you do not remember, you might refer back to the previous chapter to see how we handled this. Since we had no best times to gauge peak form by, we took our gauge of capabilities by comparing a distance common to our three speed horses, seven furlongs. Lacking an index, this was our next best yard stick.

In the 9th, only three have index times in a field of twelve. These need not worry us. Whenever we're in doubt, we can always pass the race, with or without index. Most professional speculators tend to pick and choose, anyway, developing a personal partiality to certain types of races.

In the third at G.P. (no index) we have three horses showing minus ratings; Stratmat, $-5\frac{1}{2}$; Trumpington, -4; French Coat, $-1\frac{1}{2}$. These are all three-year-olds again in this race, so we must remember to be flexible in the matter of continued improvement.

Stratmat, (5)-$(11\frac{1}{4})$-$(-5\frac{1}{2})$
Trumpington, (5)-$(-2\frac{1}{4})$-(-4)
French Coat, (1)-(5)-$(-1\frac{1}{2})$

At first glance, Trumpington seems to be the choice with the most consistent improvement. But he won his last in the best time he has shown in all his past performances. On the strength of this win, the conditions require Trumpington to pick up eight pounds. It would seem to be expecting too much of him to show further improvement right at this time, even though he did seem to handle that last one with ease, waltzing in by five lengths. He cannot be ignored in this, but neither can we play him in clear conscience.

Stratmat, of course, has the fastest rating for his last race, but that middle rating in his speed-line is unfortunate, unless we want to arbitrarily conclude he ran into a traffic problem in that one. He has shown a (-5) in a fast track $1\frac{1}{16}$, and a $(-4\frac{1}{2})$ for a fast track 6 F., and a (-6) for a heavy track race at 7 F. In this latter he outfinished Trumpington, though not by much. Both were beaten by a very small margin in this same race by French Coat. But this latter has not shown the improvement of the other two.

Trumpington is the earn-ability-class of these three, but that win in his last still bothers us. Stratmat is second in line on earn-ability-class, and he has the best rating for the last race, and also the best fast track rating. He seems to be the one to expect more improvement from in this race, but believe me no one would blame you if you elected to pass this one up.

Anyhow, Stratmat won at $14.80, an overlay if you accept our figures. Trumpington was bet to favoritism and finished second, beaten only a nose by Stratmat. French Coat was 5th.

Now, let's look at the 4th race because it presents a different kind of a problem, though each and every entrant has a best time recorded in the index. Or we should say it presents a different kind of lesson.

Devil's Image shows the best index speed with a classy 1:09⅘. The next best, with 1:10, can be thrown out of consideration, because he has gone way back since that good one. So Devil's Image stands alone, we might say, in the index. And off of the last race rating he is 5¾ points the best.

His speed-line, $(2\frac{1}{2})\text{-}(-2\frac{1}{2})\text{-}(-6\frac{1}{2})$. Nice improvement, consistent and steady. Though he is still (in that last race) 4½ points away from his best, since 1:09⅘ gets a −11 rating, still his rate of improvement has been five points from the 3rd race back to the 2nd, and four points from the 2nd race back to the last. Therefore it is not unreasonable to expect he could hit his peak and equal or better his index time, in which case he would appear to be a mortal cinch with this band.

His stablemate, Chateau, does not interest us because his speed-line indicates a steady decline since his last win at Tropical.

Poloriot, whose last race rating is second to Devil's Image

(− ¾) shows a gradual decline over his last three races (−2)-(−1½)-(−¾).

Regal Heir, though he is third with a plus ½ is so obviously erratic and devoid of class, that there is no point in wasting time on him (13¾)-(21)-(½). No competition here.

On earn-ability, however, Devil's Image is far from tops. Rip Road, with $765 per-race earn-ability, is the class, though he would not appear to be when we see how cheaply he has been running at F.G., though he improved his claiming price there with racing. He won at $3000, then $4000, just missed at $5500, then won at $6000. Then his connections brought him to Gulfstream for the better purses. And the gamble paid off, though we could hardly go for him with his plus three speed rating.

So, Devil's Image broke tardily, tenth in a ten-horse field, and while he made up ground, he finished fourth.

Rip Road won it, at $27.60, and increased his speed rating from a plus (3) to a minus (−3) and up another $1500 in claiming price.

The lesson we mentioned is that there is no such thing as a mortal cinch. Had Devil's Image broken more alertly, he might have taken Rip Road, but, in retrospect, we wonder. For Rip Road was a horse whose potential was not even known to his connections. If Devil's Image had gotten a better start and forced Rip Road's pace, he might have run as much faster as necessary to win.

While we don't run into a situation like this often, it's a good thing to keep in mind the next time we're tempted to send in the family jewels on a mortal cinch. Remember that mortal cinches can be beaten. Even Man O'War lost one.

Later, we will suggest wagering controls which will prevent us from going overboard on any one horse.

Since there is nothing more to be learned from the other races carded this day, nothing new, that is, there would be little to be gained for the student-fan by belaboring the points already made. Familiarity and facility can only come through practice, so roll out a stack of back *Forms,* or *Telegraphs* if you prefer, and go to work.

You now have the basis for intelligent selecting: 1) Awareness of the racing secretary's conditions. 2) Earn-ability-class. 3) New, comparable speed ratings. 4) Condition and the improving horse.

There are contributing factors which we will discuss in ensuing chapters, but there's no reason for you not to start practicing to become a virtuoso with what you already have to work with.

Whether you plan to become a system player, an angle player, or a handicap-analysis selector, there is no substitute for basic knowledge—and when the time comes, *experience.*

7. Consistency

Consistency can be every bit as big a headache to the unseasoned selector as was class before we supplied the pain-killer, earn-ability, and speed before the control by comparable ratings. But it is a useful factor once we learn not to let it mislead us. And, believe me, it can really send us into some blind switches if we don't watch out.

To most of the fringe-dabblers in this factor, it will doubtless come as something of a surprise to learn that there is more than one kind of consistency, and that the brand most commonly used is the most misleading.

The last time I was on the West Coast for the winter racing, I ran into this bird at Santa Anita. This affable, three-hundred-pound oracle had the world by the tail on a down-hill pull, and was anxious to impart the secret of success to any and all who came within reach of his voice, and it was practically impossible not to and stay inside the park.

Chubby had discovered consistency—or what he fondly believed was consistency. Chubby was winning, and one doesn't get anyplace arguing with a winner. In this state of anesthesia, no hoss player is going to believe Lady Luck is only building him up for a grand slam kick in the pants.

For his hot-shot, double-locked, copper-riveted mortal-cinch spot plays, Chubby figured consistency from the box score in the upper right hand corner of each set of past performances.

By the simple expedient of dividing the number of wins shown in the box score by the number of starts, he had percentage of win consistency. A nice figure to have. Interesting. But of what use is it unless that consistency was established at today's distance and over today's kind of track?

Let's put it another way. Suppose today's race is carded at five and a half furlongs and the track is fast. The beastie Chubby is going to risk his dough on has 40% win consistency. Wow! Some horse. But what Chubby doesn't know from the box score is that this hide is a marathoner and a mudder. Every one of those wins was earned at 1½ miles or more, and every one of them was on a gooey track. What price Chubby's consistency figure now?

So, I have deliberately exaggerated in order to drive home a point. This horse, sent out on a fast track, and against a reasonably capable group of five-and-a-half-furlong sprinters, could not ordinarily be expected to stand a chance. Consistency, then—that is to say win consistency, or win-and-place, or in-the-money consistency—should be figured at today's distance and on today's kind of track in order to be reliable over a period of time and not just for a short, hot run such as Chubby was enjoying.

Furthermore, consistency, even at its very best usage, should not be considered a basic factor in the sense that class, speed and present form are basic. I once made a rather lengthy breakdown of winners on the California tracks with regard to consistency alone. About fifty percent of the winners had shown reasonably good percentages. The other fifty percent had not. A stand off.

In our opinion, it should be regarded as an amplifying factor, or as a good tie-breaking factor. In other words, if we have isolated a pretty good wagering medium by the use of class, speed, and condition, and then we find he also has a good consistency percentage at today's distance and over today's kind of strip, the pretty good bet has evolved into a much sounder risk.

So, instead of using the box score to figure consistency, let's draw ours from the past performances, and if today's race is at six furlongs and the track is fast, let's consider only those races in which our contestant met these same conditions. And once we have computed this *sensible* consistency percentage, it will either amplify or detract from the contender already pointed up by the other factors. Or if we have two or three contestants that figure too close together to allow for a fair margin, and if one figures well on consistency and the other, or others do not, then consistency has been the means for breaking the tie or stalemate. In these ways, consistency is valuable.

If we are looking for selections for win play, then win consistency should be used. If we have a place set-up, then win & place consistency should be used. And if we're going to follow in the footsteps of the legendary Chicago O'Brien and play show, then in-the-money consistency will best suit our purpose, depending, of course, on how much action we want. It could be, for instance, that we want to play some extra good show spots, and we might get the idea that win consistency would be the thing to use. This would be true only if we checked far enough to ascertain that the beastie also got his full share of places and shows. High win percentage such as the 40% mentioned above does not necessarily constitute a good show betting medium, for we don't have to look far through the *Form* to discover that some horses either win or get nothing. Others are either there or thereabouts in a very high percentage of their races, but are rarely able to win. These could be excellent place or show bets which would be missed if play was based on win percentage.

I have just flipped open the *Form* for March 16, 1957. It's the 6th at Gulfstream, and right on top in post position number one is a colt named Canadian Champ. Here is his box score:

1957	4	1	1	0	$ 3,625
1956	16	10	1	0	$71,350

Last year and this year, not once has he shown up in the show hole, and only twice has he even placed, yet his win record is certainly impressive. Now let's check him in the past performances. Ten races are shown, four of which culminated in wins. This is not as good as the percentage shown in the box score, but still very good until we look at the conditions and discover this race is carded at 6½ F. Three of the wins in the past performances were at route distances, the fourth at 5½ F.

In the same race is the four-year-old colt, Singer. He had twenty-two starts in 1956, and only won one of them. But he placed four times and showed six times. We could hardly get excited over him for win play, from a consistency viewpoint, but he might be satisfactory for certain kinds of show systems.

On March 15, 1957, in the 4th at G.P. there's a four-year-old gelding named Fiddlin' Son. He has been out four times in '57, not at all in '56. Of the four starts he won once and placed twice. That's 75% win & place consistency. He ran second again—and for a $7.10 place mutuel. Oddly enough, he figured second in speed by our ratings, and second in earnability, and had showed steady improvement in the last three races. All his past performances were at either six or seven furlongs. Today's race, 6½ F.

This brings us to a broader look at figuring consistency. If we need more action than can be obtained by using only today's distance in striking our percentages, we can expand this to include all sprints if today's race is a sprint and/or all routes if today's race is a route.

Now, let's go back to that fourth race at G.P. on March 11, in which Rip Road beat out Devil's Image for the hog's share of the purse. Here we were trying to put our finger on a winner, so win consistency would have been the thing to use. Rip Road had six races at six furlongs, and on a dry track, in his past performances. Four of these culminated in wins. That's 67% win consistency.

Devil's Image, on the other hand, had three races at six furlongs, over a fast strip. None of these were winning efforts, and in only one of them was he able to show. In this case, Rip Road's high consistency amplified his better class, which we had already found by earn-ability. While this would not necessarily have influenced us to select Rip Road for play, since he had not been forced to display his speed in those cheap races at F.G., still it might have influenced us not to feel so confident about Devil's Image. Giving away both class and win consistency to a rival contestant certainly should have removed some of the mortal-cinch lustre. In the business of selecting winners, it's as important to discover a horse's deficiencies as it is to count up his virtues.

It might be just as well to develop the thought a little further concerning the relationship between class and consistency.

The length of a consistent period of racing is a yardstick to class. The classier the horse, the longer he is able to hold his form.

The horse that shows good consistency at both sprint and route distances, definitely has a touch of class, and the horse that can run well on both a fast track and in the goo certainly has a little more to offer than the hide that has to have a fast track, and/or mud in order to put his best foot forward. These things the selector can't help but notice while figuring consistency from the past performances. While it is true we take our class from earn-ability, still the more we know about a horse, the better qualified we are to arrive at a sound selection.

Consistency also tells us something of the horse's connections, in that it reflects the trainer's acumen at spotting his horse where he can do the most good. A pretty fair sort of horse can be made to look silly if his trainer hasn't the knack for spotting him in line with his capabilities.

The truth of this can be seen time and again. An inconsistent horse is Claimed and suddenly becomes the acme of consistency. Or a good, steady earner changes hands and thereafter can't seem to get within shouting distance of a purse. While this is sometimes caused by a difference in training methods, more often it is a reflection of the trainer's ability at picking good spots.

Consistency, like the other factors, must be accompanied by good form in order to mean anything. A horse that is definitely staling off might still show a good consistency figure. For instance, let's take a look at Dark Ruler in the 7th at G.P. on March 12. Since his past races are nearly all six-furlong, fast-track efforts, we'll use the box score rather than attempt to reproduce his past performances.

| 1957 | 3 | 1 | 0 | 1 | $ 2,850 |
| 1956 | 17 | 4 | 7 | 3 | $23,275 |

In twenty starts, he had five wins for 25% W.C. For win & place consistency, his percentage was 60, and it went up to 80% on an in-the-money basis. Good, much better than average. But here's his speed line: (-15)-$(-2\frac{1}{4})$-$(-1\frac{1}{4})$. That slowest speed rating was made in January (the 26th), and his connections, recognizing the symptoms, took him out of competition. Now, in March, after being rested almost two months, he is being brought back. Had he been allowed to flub along until he ran himself back in shape, unsuspecting consistency advocates like Chubby would have lost some bets needlessly, for it would take several bad races before the consistency percentages would be hurt appreciably.

Dark Ruler's good consistency percentages also strongly reflect the keen perception and ability of his trainer—no other than J. Fitzsimmons—for when brought back after being rested he won at first asking, thus adding to his record of consistency.

So, if you keep your eyes open, and stay within reasonable limits in the use of consistency as a factor, it will prove its value over and over again.

8. Impost

In view of the great stress the racing secretary and the horsemen place on *weight* (or "impost") the student-fan may wonder why we have made so little mention of it in the various examples we have used to illustrate points in selection procedure.

When we consider the emphasis placed on the weight problem by the above-mentioned worthies, it almost seems as though there is nothing left to be said on the subject. Since the weights are dictated, in a manner of speaking, by the racing secretary, who knows considerably more about the subject in all probability than we ever shall, and then are considered and either accepted as favorable or rejected as discriminatory by the horsemen who are, themselves, adept at figuring imposts, we might well be forgiven, or at least understood, if we chose not to stick our neck out on the subject at all.

However, after due consideration, we have decided there are a few remarks that can and should be made.

In the first place, the student-fan ought to have an on-sight acquaintance with the Scale of Weights, the better to understand the racing secretary's endeavors. A copy of the Scale is reproduced with this chapter. From this can be seen where certain initial weight assignments in the secretary's conditions have had their origin. It is to be hoped the student will also see why the secretary must write in certain other conditions in his endeavor to equalize the chances of each contestant.

It has always been difficult for me to see why a big strong beast, like a horse, should be affected one way or another by the addition or the removing of a pound or two of weight— unless we can believe the old story about that final one tiny straw that when added to the camel's already heavy burden broke his back.

The fact remains that weight packing ability is something that varies with each horse. Some will not race to advantage with more than, say, 112 pounds, while others will keep right on winning if burdened with 150 pounds.

It will be frequently noticed in the past performances where horse A and horse B finished close together in their last race. For the sake of illustration, let's say horse A beat horse B by a half length and that he carried five pounds more than horse B. Here they are, meeting again today. Horse A is in with two pounds more than last trip, while horse B is carrying two pounds less. In the majority of cases, often enough to create a successful system, in fact, this small shift in weight will wipe out that half-length advantage horse A enjoyed in that last race. This time, horse B will beat horse A. BUT, let's suppose these two, on their return engagement, are again weighted so that horse A is carrying just five pounds more than horse B. There may have been a change in impost, but the difference is still just five pounds.

In the majority of cases, horse A will again beat horse B.

I once knew a dispenser of spot plays in L.A. who supplied his clients with a spot only when this identical situation existed. To the best of my knowledge, he kept his clients reasonably happy.

This should bring home to all of us that the thoroughbred

is a flesh and blood creature and subject to the same weaknesses as us human critters. The difference is only a matter of degree. For instance, a comparatively light bundle, say ten pounds, carried by you or me, would not seem an intolerable burden, or slow us down noticeably as we walk home from the store, provided home is only a short walk. But if home is, say, ten blocks from the store, chances are that ten-pound bundle will appear to get heavier and heavier as we become increasingly tired.

So it is with a big, strong horse. Where the impost burden has its telling affect is not in the early stages of the race, but in the stretch when he is tired. The weight on his back that seemed little more than a feather at the start has become a mountain. This is when the freight train gets stopped.

Then what about the sensational stretch drivers who turn on those "tremendous bursts of speed" the sports scribes love to expound about? An illusion! Admittedly, he appears to be flying, but the fact of the matter is that he is running the slowest quarter of the race. Because his competition is more tired than he, he seems to have found a new reservoir of speed, but it is only that the others are slowing more rapidly than he. He is a stronger horse, better able to cope with the rapidly increasing burden on his back. Ask the pace handicapper among your friends. He will tell you the final quarter of any race is always the slowest.

So weight-packing ability is a matter of inherent strength and stamina. At the peak of his form a horse can handle more weight, successfully, than he can at any time on his way up to peak, or after he has passed it and is staling off.

Thus, right at the time when he is coming to hand and is best able to cope with weight, the conditions written by the secretary will allow him the most weight off for non-winning in the recent past while off peak form. Conversely, while at or near peak and gaining victories, his weight advantages in pounds off for non-winning are wiped out, so that at about the time when his form cycle is changing, when he has passed his peak and is staling off, he can enjoy no weight concessions until such time when he can again qualify as a non-winner "since such and such a date."

Thus, by studying and understanding the conditions, and knowing by our analysis that we have an improving horse in prospect, we may see an extra advantage not visible to the uninformed fan. So let's say we have a horse, capable of coping with 126 pounds with authority when at peak form, going to hit his peak in today's race (we know this from our improving speed ratings as compared to the index best time), and yet getting in at, maybe twelve pounds less than this because of non-winning a certain number of races since such and such a date. This makes what would normally be just a run-of-the-mill selection into a sterling opportunity to cash a mutuel ducat.

In such cases, the winner is likely to be the lightly-weighted horse, rather than the high-weight as would be the normal expectation in a handicap. By this we do not mean the high-weights never win the claiming and allowance races. Definitely, they do.

Take Jo Davis in the first at G.P. on March 15, 1957. Top weight is called out in the conditions as 122 pounds. Since Jo Davis is a four-year-old filly, and is racing against horses, colts and geldings, she's entitled to five pounds off this top impost. At 117 pounds, then, she is considered top-weighted with the males and geldings carrying 122 pounds.

This race is for non-winners in 1957 with weight off for non-winners since November 27. But Jo Davis won two in December at Tropical, so has to pack top weight for fillies.

SCALE OF WEIGHTS

The Scale of Weights reproduced herewith has been adopted unanimously by the Racing Associations of Canada, Mexico, and the United States with the exceptions of California and Louisiana, where certain changes have been made. These exceptions are noted.

Dist.	Age	Jan.	Feb.	Mar. & Apr.	May	Jun.	Jul.	Aug.	Sep.	Oct.	Nov. & Dec.
	2-yr	...	...	86	87	92	93	98	105	107	109
	3-yr	112	113	115	116	117	119	121	123	124	125
½ M.	4-up	126	126	126	126	126	126	126	126	126	126
Calif.	2-yr	...	...	100	100	100	100	100	105	107	109
La.	2-yr	...	...	...	...	...	...	...	...	...	109
	3-yr	116	116	116	...	...	...	...	...	...	125
	4-up	126	126	126	...	...	...	...	...	...	126
	2-yr	...	...	84	90	95	98	102	105	108	111
	3-yr	114	115	116	119	120	122	123	125	126	127
	4-yr	130	130	130	130	130	130	130	130	130	130
¾ M.	5-up	132	132	132	132	132	130	130	130	130	130
Calif.	2-yr	...	...	100	100	100	100	102	105	108	111
La.	2-yr	...	...	...	...	...	...	...	...	...	111
	3-yr	115	115	115	...	...	...	...	...	...	127
	4-yr	130	130	130	...	...	...	...	...	...	130
	5-up	132	132	132	...	...	...	...	...	...	130
	2-yr	...	...	...	...	...	...	...	95	97	100
1 M.	3-yr	105	107	109	112	114	116	118	119	120	120
	4-yr	124	126	128	127	126	126	126	126	126	126
	5-up	127	128	129	128	127	126	126	126	126	126
Calif.	2-yr	...	...	...	...	...	...	...	100	100	100
La.	2-yr	...	...	...	...	...	...	...	...	...	100
	3-yr	110	110	110	...	...	...	...	...	...	120
	4-yr	127	127	127	...	...	...	...	...	...	126
	5-up	129	129	129	...	...	...	...	...	...	126
	2-yr	...	...	...	...	...	...	...	93	95	98
	3-yr	102	104	106	108	112	114	117	118	120	120
1¼	4-yr	124	126	128	127	126	126	126	126	126	126
	5-up	127	128	129	128	127	126	126	126	126	126
Calif.	2-yr	...	...	...	...	...	...	...	100	100	100
La.	2-yr	...	...	...	...	...	...	...	...	...	98
	3-yr	105	105	105	...	...	...	...	...	...	120
	4-yr	127	127	127	...	...	...	...	...	...	126

Dist.	Age	Jan.	Feb.	Mar. & Apr.	May	Jun.	Jul.	Aug.	Sep.	Oct.	Nov. & Dec.
	5-up	129	129	129	...	...	...	...	...	...	126
	3-yr	99	101	103	105	107	110	116	118	119	120
	4-yr	124	126	127	127	126	126	126	126	126	126
1½ M.	5-up	126	127	128	128	127	126	126	126	126	126
Calif.	3-yr	100	101	103	105	107	110	116	118	119	120
La.	3-yr	105	105	105	...	...	...	...	...	...	120
	4-yr	127	127	127	...	...	...	...	...	...	126
	5-up	129	129	129	...	...	...	...	...	...	126
	3-yr	96	98	100	102	104	108	112	114	117	118
	4-yr	122	125	127	126	126	126	125	125	126	126
2 M.	5-up	125	127	129	128	127	126	125	125	124	124
Calif.	3-yr	100	100	100	102	104	108	112	114	117	118
La.	3-yr	100	100	100	...	...	...	...	...	...	118
	4-yr	126	126	126	...	...	...	...	...	...	124
	5-up	128	128	128	...	...	...	...	...	...	124

It will be noted that there is no mention of sex allowance for fillies and mares. This is something understood among horsemen. It is never mentioned in the racing secretary's condition book, either, but always understood and allowed.

Since her last win, on December 27, Jo Davis had not been impressive. She had raced three times, and had been no closer than fifth in any of them, though not badly beaten from a standpoint of lengths. In fact, in her last two, she had closed ground in the run to the wire, with 119 pounds and 116 pounds respectively. This would indicate she was not too far off form. So out of curiosity, we checked. We compared ratings, her last race against her last winning race at Tropical. Her last race was ¾ length faster than her last winning race. She had her form, but it wasn't obvious to the casual observer because she had been running against a higher grade of claimers since her last win. To one in possession of this knowledge, it should have come as no real surprise when she took this one and paid the handsome mutuel of $32.20.

The point we are trying to drive home is that, for the most part, the weight problem is very competently handled by the conditions. If we, the selectors, are alert enough to spot a sharp horse, properly placed as to distance and track condition, we need have little concern about his ability to handle his weight assignment, especially if his past performances show that he has handled a similar package creditably at one time or another.

Looking at Jo Davis again, we see she carried 116 pounds to a three-length, easy victory in that last winning effort at Tropical. It would be unrealistic to have doubts about her ability to cope with one more, 117 pounds, today. Rock Dozer, with 122 pounds, was made a slight favorite in the betting. He had carried 121 in his last race and missed only by a head to Gwenys Kin who is not entered in this race. He had closed 4½ lengths in the run to the wire with that 121 burden so it would be not unreasonable to suppose he could handle the 122 pound assignment today. *But*—the second horse in the betting of today's race, Reighbout, (only 10¢ difference between his odds and Rock Dozer's) is in with 119, a package we cannot assume from his past races he can cope with. It is true he ran third with 115 pounds, but he was backing up.

Doubtless the dear public overlooked this shortcoming because Arcaro was in the boot.

In any case, Jo Davis won it in a photo. Rock Dozer was second again, by a nose this time, and Reighbout was third, a coupla lengths farther back.

This sort of weight comparison often pays off, whereas the selector who automatically makes an adjustment in his figures, for weight on and/or off, (such as three pounds equal to one length) is indulging in a self-hoax. A package that could "stop" one horse would not faze another, so to assume that every horse would react identically to an automatic speed adjustment for pounds on or off of that last race, or the one used to qualify him, is utter folly. A horse, too inherently slow to match strides with the anticipated pace in today's race is not going to be helped to overcome this basic lack by a light-weight assignment. Nor is a feather going to be a worthy sub-stitute for an inherent lack of class. And most certainly of all, a light impost cannot compensate for a deficiency in present form.

On the other hand, if our selection has the speed, class, and form to do today's job, and has demonstrated his ability to carry weights reasonably close to today's assignment, or has demonstrated his aptitude for handling increasingly heavy impost, even though he has not carried today's weight before, we have little to worry about except the fickleness of Lady Luck, such as a jockey-goof or an unfavorable traffic pattern.

So let's be realistic about weight. If we are accurate in our evaluation of the other factors, we can tell almost at a glance if the weight factor is unfavorable.

9. Favorable Percentages

In the opening chapter we stated very emphatically that the races *can* be beaten. In this chapter we are going to discuss the mathematics behind this contention, for we believe it is vital to eventual success for the student-fan to have confidence in what he is doing. The man who cannot beat the races is the one who relies on luck instead of cold, hard figures. Actually, he belongs to the school of sad-faced characters who claim the races can't be beaten. Yet he believes *he* will beat them because of a special deal with Lady Luck. But she is a fickle babe. She might take you by the hand today, but she'll drop you flat tomorrow.

The seasoned speculator plays for percentages. He knows what his percentages and averages are going to be over a given period of time. He knows better than to count on any one race, any one day, or any one week. But because he has carefully built his method of operation to get the percentages working for him, he is never in doubt about the eventual outcome. He even knows within a percentage point or two what his profit will be for a given period of time.

Please note we are talking about the serious speculator, not the sensational plunger of the Diamond Jim Brady ilk. It is these latter birds who are colorful copy for the scribes. It is they, also, who die broke. The quiet, conservative speculator doesn't make the headlines, nor does he want to. He's too busy making a good living in his chosen field.

He has absolutely nothing in common with the caricatures in Damon Runyon's immortal fiction, nor is he a counterpart of the stereotyped psychopath traditionally presented by Hollywood as a typical horse player. You won't recognize him as a type at the track, or away from it.

In what ways, then, does the Turf differ from other forms of speculation, or, if you will, outright gambling?

Perhaps the most thorough approach is an understanding of the parimutuel method of wagering, and it is truly startling how few fans know its workings.

All money poured into the mutuel machines for each race is pooled. At no time is the management covering your bet. Their function is that of stakes holder—and tax collector. All money bet to win goes into a *win* pool; all of it bet to place goes into a *place* pool; and all show money goes into the *show* pool. The Daily Double pool is a separate operation altogether and has no connection whatever with the straight, place, and show wagering.

The approximate odds flashed on the totalisator board at intervals, after wagering starts, are a direct reflection of the amounts being played by the wagering public on the various contestants. The shortest odds on the board means that more money has been bet on this horse to *win* than on any other. And that longest long-shot shown represents the smallest corner of the pool.

Since the management is only the stakesholder and is not covering your bet, they don't care what horse, or horses, you bet on; how little or how much you play; or whether you win or lose. Some managements, however, do recommend to the fans that they should not bet more than they can afford to lose.

This, of course, is sound advice and is intended solely for the welfare of the fans.

Simultaneously with the springing of the starting gate which gets the field away and running, the parimutuel windows, or the electronic machines behind them, lock, and the final totals are recorded by the totalisator.

First the Win pool. From the total amount of money bet into this pool, the "bite" or "take" is extracted. This is 15% in Florida, 13% in California, and as low as 10% at certain other tracks across the country. Approximately half of this goes to the State in the form of tax, the other portion going to the track to help defray purses and/or other operating expenses and to supply the track with its profit.

Now, from the residue left in the pool, an amount equal to the total bet on the winning horse is subtracted, since the law states that the full amount wagered must be returned to a successful bettor. The remaining money left in the pool is then divided by the equivalent of the total number of $2.00 win tickets purchased on the ultimate winner. This gives the amount of profit per two-dollar bet. To this is added the two dollars wagered and the total recorded in lights on the tote board.

Thus, if the ultimate winner went off at 3/1, the profit on the bet would be $6.00, plus the return of the original wager, making the gross return, or payoff, $8.00.

In case of a dead heat, the win pool is handled like a place pool, which we will now look into.

Here again, the "take" or "bite" is extracted from the total amount bet into the place pool on all contestants. Then the amounts bet on both horses that figured in the place (the winner and the second horse), are deducted from the pool. This remainder is then halved and the equivalent of the total number of two dollar tickets for each is divided into his half, thus getting the net profit per two-dollar wager for each. To clarify this, let's say each half of the pool remainder is one thousand dollars. Horse A that figured in the place (the winner) had the equivalent of 500 two-dollar tickets bought on him. The net profit, then would be $2.00 and the payoff, $4.00.

The horse that ran second, we'll say, was a longshot. He had only the equivalent of 100 two-dollar tickets bought on him. The net profit, then, would be ten dollars, and the gross return, or payoff, $12.00.

It will be seen that we cannot tell in advance what a place or show payoff will be, as we can in the case of a winner, because it depends entirely which horses, and how many tickets there are out against them, as to how much pool money will be available to whack up between the successful ones.

In the show pool, after the bite is extracted, and the total amount of money bet on the three successful ones subtracted, the remaining money in the pool is divided three ways, equally among the three horses figuring in the show—the winner, the second horse and the third horse. The payoff on each, then, will be in direct proportion to the equivalent of the number of two-dollar show tickets purchased on each.

If a dead heat should occur for the show position, then the third of the pool set aside for figuring the profit for the show wager is divided equally between the two horses figuring in the dead heat for show. This does not affect the shares for the winning horse and the horse that finished second. And in case of a dead heat for second, a half of a half of the available place pool is allotted each horse in the dead heat and does not affect the portion for the horse that won.

It will be seen from this that the payoffs, which are never standard and inflexible as are the payoffs at a gaming house where you always know in advance what you will get if your play turns out successfully. You also know, unless you are woefully uninformed, that the management is covering your bets, and that the odds and the house "take" have all been figured out in advance so that management's profit is inevitable. Yes, we're talking about an honestly run house. Therefore, since there are only one hundred cents in a dollar, where is your profit to come from? That's right, you've got to have a hot run. You've got to be shot full of luck, because there's no honest way you can get the percentages working with you. And when that fickle babe, Lady Luck, moves on, you've had it, unless you happen to have sense enough to quit while ahead— and who does?

You may argue that the "bite" at the tracks is larger than the "house take" at a gambling joint. It is. But the prices are fixed at a gambling hell. They are static. And they are not quite enough, with the "house take," for you to break even on flat bets. And when you can't show a small profit on flat bets, there's no progression yet devised that will produce anything but financial suicide.

Why wouldn't this be even more true at the tracks where the "bite" is bigger? Because the prices are not fixed or static. They are fluid at all times, subject to the mass whim of the betting public, and the betting public is right less than a third of the time. The national win percentage for bet favorites is approximately 32% year in and year out, and the average payoff less than $6.00. In fact, 6% of them go at even money or less. The dear public, when it thinks it's got its teeth into something good, will bleed it to death. The resulting underlay will get nobody well.

An underlay is a horse that is bet down below his chances of winning. He is, to put it another way, the very opposite of a bargain. Anyone betting an underlay is paying too much for his two-buck ticket.

This, then, is one way we, the parimutuel bettors, can help get the percentages on our side. We can refuse to accept underlaid prices. If our carefully arrived at selection is bet down too far, say below three to one (3/1), we simply refuse to risk our money. We watch this one, or we go get a hot dog. If, however, our next selection, in the next race, which we exercised just as much care with, goes postward at 3/1 or higher, we get aboard. Thus, our winners always pay a minimum of $8.00 and frequently a great deal more.

Do you remember the example of Duke's Sandal being made an utterly false favorite (see Chapter 5) and our legitimate selection, On Her Way, being *overlaid* at 9/2 as a result? At $11.40, our profit on this one play would have been a yield of 470% on invested capital. With opportunities like that 68% of the time, need we worry about a 15% "bite"? It's good for the morale to gripe about high "bite" and income taxes, but we pay them, and manage to keep right on eating.

So let's indulge in a little elementary mathematics. Let's reconsider that 32% winning favorites and let's give them an average value of $6.00 which they never attain. Thirty-two winners out of a hundred at six dollars gives us a grand total of $182.00, which would be gross return. Since we had to make one hundred bets at $2.00 per bet, our investment would be $200.00 or a net loss of $18.00.

On the other hand, if we make one hundred plays, accepting only those of our selections which are overlooked by the public by at least 3/1, and even assuming we were able to cash winning ducats only 30% of the time, we would have a gross return of $240.00, or a net profit of $40.00. This is a yield of 20% on invested capital. And, so help me, if you can't do *better* than that after exposure to this book, you're going to break my heart.

The foregoing example doesn't mean this is the only way of getting the percentages working for you—or even the best. It was used, simply, to illustrate how very simple it is at the track to break out of the barrier on top. Whether you stay there or not depends on several imponderables—chiefly the individual speculator's emotional stability.

Another simple way to get the percentages on your side is with those very win underlays we discarded just a moment ago. No, I'm not nuts. The even money to odds-on win underlays win approximately 55% of their races. Following this kind of action will produce an annual loss of about 5%. But backing these same horses to place, and they win or run second nearly ninety percent of the time, will result in an annual *profit* of some 5%. Backing the show on this action will result in some 3% annual profit. The answer to this seeming paradox is simple. When the win end is heavily underlaid, the place and show are usually overlaid—that is, allowed to go postward at better odds than their chances would indicate.

Usually, however, I prefer to follow my own selections regardless of the betting action, for it has been my experience that the betting public will overlay my pix more than twice as often as they underlay them. Also, by sticking strictly to my own pix, and ignoring the tote board, I avoid the false favorites the bettors have such a quaint habit of creating. Even some of the heavily bet down underlays are utterly false and should not be enjoying even a lukewarm favoritism. Thus the win percentage among the very short-priced variety goes up to a point where it is possible to take a profit on the others.

Another way the fan can get the percentages working for him is to play more than one horse in a race when the odds warrant it. For instance, in those races particularly where our analysis shows two or more contestants figuring too close together to separate we often find the public engaged in its favorite pastime of creating a false favorite and thus letting our tied good ones go at overlaid odds, high enough, in fact, so that we can bet both or all three of ours, and still enjoy a nice profit no matter which one wins.

Some hard-heads go into a state of shock if we suggest play-

ing more than one horse to win, but we will develop several
such systems, profitable ones, a little later on which should
prove to the most skeptical that it can be done.

There is an axiom around the tracks which goes like this:
In order to beat the races, you have to beat the price. Actually,
this is just another way of saying you have to beat the percentages, get them working for you.

Let's say you want to be a show player, and don't look
down your nose at show. There is lots to be said for it—and
Chicago O'Brien made a few million dollars show betting. A
smaller capital is needed to play show than would be needed
to play the same selections to win. The frequency of the payoffs are a big advantage, if not an absolute *must,* for certain
kinds of temperaments. There is the added safety factor in
those close finishes, the ones we always seem to get photoed
out of on the win end. And you can get the percentages working with you just as easily on the show end as the win.

For instance, if you find your method is producing an average payoff of about $3.00, it doesn't take a mathematical
genius to arrive at the conclusion that, to show a flat bet profit,
we're going to have to have about 70% of our selections show.
That would be minimum. If we've been playing bet favorites,
we're about 5% short since these show only about 65% on a
national average. That means we have to either get an increase
in the number of hits or a better average show price. Or both.
A breakdown of the work we have done will show us which
have been the weakest plays. By eliminating this type of play,
we will beef up both hit percentage and average payoff, and
we're in business.

I don't mean to over-simplify this, but I do want to get the
idea across that it can be done by the application of a little
horse sense. Any system you may be using which almost, but
not quite, keeps you out of the red, can be analyzed and
strengthened, if you bring the proper objectivity to the chore.

And it can be done because the price in horse racing is a very flexible and variable thing, virtually controlled by a lot of enthusiastic but misinformed, or uninformed, people who know a lot less about what they are doing than you do—now that you have come this far with your studies.

Sometimes your system just fails because you have the cart before the horse. The ingredients may be perfectly sound but are being applied in the wrong order. This is so startlingly true and important that we're going to present a full chapter on this chronology factor alone. At that time, we will take at least one system, a weak one, and subject it to a search for chronology. We will rearrange the factors, the very same ones used in the weak system, and come up with a really potent selection medium.

We have no such opportunity at the gambling house, where the prices and the types of play are static. A hot run of luck is our only chance there, but luck has nothing to do with our success or failure at the track, and the reason we *can* come out ahead consistently is because the price is there for us to take, once we learn how to coax the percentages around to working *for* us instead of *against* us.

10. Handicap-Analysis

So now we're ready to start applying what we have been discussing toward the pleasurable business of making an honest bob at the track.

In order to gain facility in the use of all the various factors and contributing considerations, let's first build our handicap-analysis procedure into as flexible a pattern as possible for convenient and productive use. While this will be of special interest to the aspiring analysts, it should also be followed carefully by the future system players, for the more we know about our subject generally, the better use we'll make of our systems later.

Though the analyst does not consider himself a system player, he is almost certain to follow a systematic procedure in the use of the various factors. In this sense he is a system player, but where the usual system will be developed around one or two of the factors, the analyst uses all of them. His work is more detailed and drawn out. Conversely, the main advantage of the system is that it eliminates some of the analyst's tedious work, and usually makes cut and dried rules which remove the necessity for the user to rely on personal judgement, for this is one department where many find themselves wanting. To be coldly and accurately analytical under severe pressure is something which requires a high percentage of ice water in the veins.

If your personal judgement is good, and unwavering under fire, then you are probably cut out to be an analyst. There is no doubt that more flexibility and versatility is available to the analyst, though we plan to offer greater elasticity than ever before in our systems also.

The first step in our handicap-analysis there should be no deviating from—a perusal and digestion of the racing secretary's conditions. This could lead to the decision as to what factor, or factors, will bear special stressing and/or which should be used to isolate the real contenders of the group.

In spite of the racing secretary's best efforts, in almost every race there will be a few horses that have no chance in this particular company—except in the biased opinion of their owners. If by studying the conditions, we can ascertain, roughly, which these are, we can eliminate a certain amount of non-productive work. Not that we recommend to any serious student that he allow himself to become parsimonious in allotting time to making his selections. Nor do we recommend his doing unnecessary work.

The legendary Pittsburgh Phil is reported to have spent an average of fifteen to sixteen hours a day on his analysis. He was not a system player, but a classifier of horses, and he kept voluminous records for this purpose. In his day, there was no *Daily Racing Form* or *New York Telegraph* to make his task easier. In fact, his biographers are of the opinion that his work and resulting records were the forerunners of the *Form* and *Telegraph*.

Be that as it may, there can be no doubt his efforts paid off, for he left behind him an estate of $1,700,000.00 when he forsook this vale of tears for wherever horse players go. If he had any secret formula, other than unstinting hard work, he took it with him.

So we have read the conditions for the first race we're going to operate on, and now the flexibility of our pattern comes into play. According to what we have learned from the conditions will come our decision whether to separate contenders by earn-ability-class, or speed. For our desire is to know which of these horses has the greatest potential. Then from this group we will determine the one, if any, in proper shape to display his wares. This we accomplish by Index comparison and improvement shown over recent races. Then will come our final separation, if any is required.

Since we cannot lay down a lot of rules for a handicap-analysis procedure without being accused of trying to make a system out of it, let's work out a block of races, step by step, making certain points and recommendations as we go along as guide posts, not as hard and fast rules. In other words, I'll attempt to show how I do it, and from this the student-analyst will form his own procedural habits, and his own pet likes and dislikes. This is inevitable. Even in system play where the rules are cut and dried, a fan will employ, either consciously or subconciously, certain of his own leanings where a close decision must be made.

Let's go to work. Since we plan to make a one-month work-out of this procedure to accompany this chapter for comparison by the student with his own results, and since this month will be February, 1957, let's start our work with the first race on February 1, 1957 at Hialeah. Later we will shift to Sunshine Park for this same period of time to bring home to the Student the striking difference possible between two winter operations, for Hialeah and Sunshine Park are at the top and the bottom of the quality ladder in so far as winter racing in Florida is concerned. From this parallel, we hope to demonstrate the importance of elasticity of viewpoint and instill in the student a healthy confidence in the adaptability of our flexible procedure.

The first race at Hialeah on February 1, 1957, was a route and a claimer. Here are the Conditions:

1⅛ MILES (Spartan Valor-Feb. 9, 1952-1:47⅕-4-118) Purse, $3,500. 4-year-olds and upward. Claiming. Weight, 124 lbs. Non-winners twice since November 27 allowed 3 lbs; a race, 6 lbs. Claiming price, $4,500; 2 lbs. for each $250 to $4,000.

A quick glance at the entrants' imposts shows us that none is carrying top weight, so all are immediately held suspect from both a class and condition standpoint. And furthermore, since speed is not as important in a route, perhaps, as it is in a sprint, this is our logical medium of separation here rather than the factor on which to pin our final decision.

In striking our speed ratings, remember, we will rate from standards on the most recent race in the horse's past performances regardless of distance or track condition, though our track is fast today. If we have to rate from an inconclusive distance or a track condition contrary to today's, it is only to get a general line on our contestants. Later we will search for ability at today's distance and today's kind of racing strip. Also, we want that most recent race to be recent enough to mean something, and here again, we must be flexible and use horse sense. While fifteen days is a good general yardstick, we have to take into consideration the fact that Hialeah usually has some 3,000 racers on the grounds, hence longer periods between opportunities to race. So, we feel impelled to stretch the fifteen days to thirty here, and trust that the trainer will keep his horse at peak on the training track.

In this way we eliminate Royal Pursuit (7); Tarcill (16); Rare Vintage (3); Antigua (8); One More Nance (30), & Swoop Down (5). King's Charger, Blue Boy, Affton King, Caboose, and Fat Boy were scratched.

We kept the contenders showing minus speed ratings, which you will remember are faster than the plus ratings. Our contenders, then are; Virginian ($-\frac{1}{2}$); Setubal (-12); For Free ($-5\frac{1}{2}$); Mark's Puzzle (-3); and Terrapin (-5).

Incidentally, this is an average group of contenders. If I were going to lay down a rule covering the number of contenders to isolate, it would be five, since the winner will be found in the first five, eighty-five percent of the time. It's a nice, round figure to base a system on. And maybe we'll do just that a little farther on.

Of these five we see almost at once that we must discard Terrapin, since nowhere in his past performances does he show any evidence that he is anything but a sprinter. He has one race at a mile, in which he took a terrific shellacking, while he won one at six furlongs and ran third at five and a half furlongs.

It is time to figure our earn-ability, and this need be done on only the remaining contenders. However, there is no law that says you can't take a look at the others if there is any doubt in your mind about that first go-round discard. In fact, it might be well to do this to convince yourself the right ones have been eliminated. This builds confidence.

Here they are: Royal Pursuit, $90; Tarcill, $91; Rare Vintage $362; Virginian, $342; Setubal, $478; One More Nance, $219; Antigua, $296; For Free, $215; Swoop Down, $273; Mark's Puzzle, $334; and Terrapin, $420.

It might appear that Rare Vintage should have rated better on speed, but checking back on his past performances. we find nothing to indicate worthwhile speed (for this band) so must conclude his trainer has been successful at spotting him in slow races in the past. He is still a discard. Terrapin, while getting a good earn-ability figure, is still a sprinter in a $1\frac{1}{8}$-mile route. Out he goes. In addition, we now look upon For Free's ($-5\frac{1}{2}$) off of that $1\frac{3}{16}$-mile race with suspicion. His other routes do not substantiate it. And his low earn-ability is at variance with this kind of indicated speed.

We said speed was an indication of class a while back. So it looks like For Free turned on the heat just that once, for the poor grade of track he comes from (six races at Wod. and Wdb., and not a single win even in that poor company) says the class figure is more accurate than the speed figure, or we should say, more representative.

So we now have three contenders left: Virginian, Setubal, and Mark's Puzzle.

Virginian shows nothing longer than 1⅟16 miles in his past performances, and shows no index time, so he is a doubtful quantity at today's distance.

Setubal has high earn-ability and the best speed rating (-12) off of that heavy race at today's distance in his last. And this race, incidentally, is the one given in the Index as his best time. Setubal is an 8-year-old horse. We cannot expect him to improve this race or even equal it to-day. Also his (-12) was made on an "off" track, and the strip is fast today. Checking back on his most recent fast track races, one at 1⅟16 and the other at 1¼ (*about* a mile and a quarter at Tropical), we find he earned a (-1) and ($-1½$) respectively. This seems to be his forte in the fast going.

Mark's Puzzle earned his (-3) on a fast track 1⅛ seven days previous to today (Jan. 25, 1957, at Hia.). He *won* this race, but in six points slower time than his best race, a (-9) at Belmont. His speed-line, while not a perfect example, is definitely indicative of an improving horse. This looks like an excellent chance for further improvement and a repeat win.

However, we'll carry our analysis a bit farther. We can gain no help or comfort from the consistency factor since these hides just don't show it. So let's invoke a point we raised earlier in the text. We stated that a horse's class is subject to change, that it could vary with distance, and with track change such as from fast to "off" and vice versa, but the biggest variation is in direct proportion to his degree of recent form —or lack of it.

Let's see if we can gain anything by inquiring into the *recent* class of Setubal and Mark's Puzzle, our two remaining serious contenders.

Setubal has been out three times in 1957. Of these three, he managed to show once, and his cut of the purse was $300. This makes his present earn-ability-class only $100 per race.

Mark's Puzzle has been out twice in 1957. He won one of these and his purse money was $2,275. This is a present earn-ability-class of $1,137 per race.

With this startling difference in *recent* Class (the next closest is Virginian with $475 per race) Mark's Puzzle emerges as the logical winner, especially since he gets in with one pound less than he carried in his last, which he won. This is the same weight he carried at Belmont when he established the best time shown in the index.

He was made a lukewarm favorite in the betting (2.75 to 1), with Rare Vintage second choice at 3.90 to 1, and Setubal third choice at 3.95 to 1.

Virginian (6.80 to 1) set all the pace right into the stretch where he gave way to Mark's Puzzle but managed to hang on for second. Rare Vintage was soundly beaten fourth, and Setubal finished way back yonder in seventh place.

Mark's Puzzle paid $7.50, 4.20, and 3.00 across the board. Improved his speed to (-8).

THE SECOND RACE

6 FURLONGS (Jet Action-Feb. 29, 1956-1:09-5-120). Purse, $3,500. 3-year-olds that have not started for a claiming price of less than $3,000 since September 1, 1956, unless a winner for a claiming price of $3,000 or more since above date. Claiming. Weight, 122 lbs. Non-winners twice since November 27 allowed 3 lbs.; a race, 6 lbs. Claiming price, $5,000.

This stacks up as a race to regard with utmost caution. It is the second half of the Daily Double and a stinker, as such loose conditions as the racing secretary wrote here would be bound to attract a pretty uncertain lot. Three maidens get into this mixed company under the conditions, and no less than half of the field of twelve have not raced within the past six weeks, and most of them not since last summer or early fall. Form is going to be hard to figure here.

There seems to be no choice of starting point in this one, but some effort has been made to contain the class of competition, so let's see if earn-ability will buy us anything interesting.

Daddy's Dasher, Guided Tour, Wedded Wife, and Daddy-kins were scratched.

Before we go any farther, let it be understood that in actual operation, we would probably not waste any more time on this one. But since we are trying to learn handicap-analysis, and must therefore face all the various kinds of races, both good and bad, for practice, even if only to learn what to avoid, let's see if we can make heads or tails of this pig race. This is the kind of race that ages the public selector before his time.

There are three horses which have much the best earn-ability-class: Tender Morsel, $965; Salmative, $860; and Kismiss, $840; with Mi Model a fringe possibility at $600 approximately.

Of these Tender Morsel has not raced since September, 1956; Salmative has not raced since December 13, 1956, which is two days outside our six-week limit. Kismiss has had two races within the six-week limit. Her speed rating in the second last race was (18) and (2½) in her last, only two weeks ago. Mi Model had a three-race speed-line of (14)-(9)-(9). With that kind of speed, or rather slow motion, and an outer fringe class, we lose interest in Mi Model, but we are slightly interested in Salmative, even though he hasn't been in competition lately. His class is one of the top three. His consistency is good, with four wins out of thirteen starts in 1956 (in sprints), and he has a 1:13⅘ workout, handily, for the six furlongs, as recently as January 27, five days ago. His speed rating for that December 13th race was (4¾).

Going back to Kismiss, with her substantial improvement in her last over the previous good class, and even better consistency (three wins in seven starts), we might have isolated a fairly sound play if it weren't for the fact that at least half of the field cannot be considered because they have not raced recently enough. This makes it an unsound betting medium and should be passed. And this is where we have it over the public selector. We don't *have* to pick for this kind of race. He is required to pick for them all. But you twisted our arm, so we have no choice but to express a preference for Kismiss.

The race was won by Riz. This filly had gone postward once in 1957, but it gave us no line on her as she lost her rider somewhere between the half-mile pole and the turn for home. Kismiss ran second and Salmative third. The betting public made Salmative a 3/2 favorite. Kismiss they let go at 10/1. She paid $10.90 for the place, and $5.50 for the show.

THIRD RACE

3 FURLONGS (Nursery Course) (Straightaway, chute) (Make Swing-Feb. 23, 1949-:32⅖-2-119). Purse $3,500. 2-year-olds, non-winners of two races. Weight, 122 lbs. Maidens allowed 5 lbs.

Speed is the answer in these baby races at the extremely short distances. Weight means practically nothing in these shorties. And since they've only been eligible to race since the first of January, there is no question of recentness, if they've raced at all. In this one, only a single entry is going to the post for the first time.

Speed, then, will be our final clincher, with earn-ability the means to isolate the contenders. Edliss and Quizzer have each won their only outings. Each earned $2,275 for that one race. There were four other winners, Strolling Sam, Miss E.K., Jimmer, and Djebet, but they had won much cheaper events. ($1,550) So, we apply the speed test to Edliss and Quizzer. Edliss got home free in 33⅕ seconds; Quizzer in 33⅖ seconds. Edliss is definitely the play, though not a mortal cinch in spite of superior class and speed, for two-year-olds are inclined to run greenly. So keep the family "jools" in the safe and just make an ordinary flat bet.

Edliss was made the 3/2 favorite, and converted for his supporters for a $5.20, 3.50, 2.60 across the board Mutuel. Jimmer, the third choice, was second, and Quizzer, 2nd in the betting, finished third.

FOURTH RACE

1³⁄₁₆ MILES (turf) (Parnassus-Feb. 17, 1954-1:55⅖-4-111) Purse, $4,000. 4-year-olds and upward. Claiming. Weight, 124 lbs. Non-winners on the turf in 1957 allowed 3 lbs.; a race December 2, 6 lbs. Claiming price $5,000.

When in doubt, start with the basic factor, class, but we have a notion, from the wording of the conditions, that we might do some good by looking for a fast, main-track effort by a horse that has a respectable turf course race somewhere back in his past performances. Our constant search for price, the possible sleeper, or overlooked horse, that prompts us here. Anyhow, first we'll break it down for earn-ability.

We come up with six possible contenders: My Friend, $518; Noble Bullet, $720; South Florida, $364; True Bruce, $319; Le Page II, $445; and Overland, $322.

In working up earn-ability, we can't help but notice the lack of consistency in the box score, for all but two horses. These two are My Friend, and Noble Bullet.

My Friend, when we turn our attention away from the box score and onto the past performances, shows three wins at

route distances out of eight starts. This is 38% win consistency. Very good, and the only race at a sprint distance, a 7½
F., was on the turf course (tc), in which he ran second,
close up.

Noble Bullet has two wins in seven fast track routes in his
past performances. This is 29% win consistency, and he does
not show a (tc) event at any distance.

Already the finger of analysis is pointing to My Friend
except for Class where Noble Bullet seems to enjoy a certain
superiority until we check for *present* class. Each horse has
raced once in 1957, at routes, and on fast strips. Off of the
1957 races, then, My Friend's earn-ability becomes $2,275
as against $275 for Noble Bullet. So, Class no longer stops
us, but something else does. My Friend won that last good
race for a (−11), and there is no index to help us decide his
chances to repeat. After scanning the route performances, his
fastest previous race seems to have been at 1¹⁄₁₆ miles in
which he ran a (−8). From this we must conclude My Friend
reached a new speed peak in his last race and it would, therefore, be a risky gamble to expect him to excel it, or even equal
it today. Nor can we go for Noble Bullet now, knowing that
he is actually far below My Friend on recent speed (only
−1½ for Noble Bullet) and the big difference in *present*
class. And none of the others we qualified on earn-ability show
anything interesting.

The race should be passed, but if you want to gamble, My
Friend would seem to be the one.

Le Page II was made the favorite in the betting, and finished
"down the track." My Friend was second choice in the betting
and, though off to a bad start (eleventh in a twelve-horse
field), ran over horses to get up for second, though he was
unable to overhaul the cheap though fleet Manormouse. (He
had a −11¼ for a 1⅛ main-track race at Tropical, though
he showed nothing to indicate he was ready to duplicate it in

this race.) Sometimes it's like that, but not often enough to keep us out of the chips.

My Friend paid $4.90 for the place and $3.90 for the show. Manormouse, entered with Mighty Impulse, paid $10.60 to win.

FIFTH RACE

This is a 6 F. sprint and would appear to lend itself best to an initial speed separation.

6 FURLONGS (Jet Action-Feb. 29, 1956-1:09-5-120) Purse, $4,500. 4-year-olds and upward. Claiming. Weight, 126 lbs. Non-winners since January 16 allowed 3 lbs.; December 10, 5 lbs.; November 20, 8 lbs. Claiming price, $12,000; 4 lbs. for each $1,000 to $10,000.

This is a high-grade claimer which should beckon to some pretty fair speedsters, which is why we elect to make our selection of contenders on speed. We feel that any of these so-called slow class horses will not stand a chance here. Mind you, we do not concede that there is any such thing as a "slow class horse." If he is slow at the moment, it is because he's off-form, and if this is so, he is not *at present* a class horse. Those others that appear slow and yet have reasonably good earn-ability owe their appearance of having class to the skill of their trainer at spotting them in slow company. In real classy, fast company, they wouldn't stand a chance. If we made our initial separation on earn-ability, we'd only have to throw the slow ones out anyway. It is a question of chronology, which we will study in detail later in connection with system play.

These showed the best last race speed: Cosmonaut (-15); Tocsin, (-8); Fresh Meadow, ($-10\frac{1}{4}$); and Lady Elliott, ($-8\frac{1}{4}$).

We shelve Cosmonaut and Lady Elliott because they have **less than half the earn-ability of Fresh Meadow and Tocsin.**

Also, Cosmonaut is primarily a router, though he won one slow (0) 6 F. race at C.D. Lady Elliott, while a fairish sprinter, doesn't show too much in her past performances, having placed twice and showed once in her last eight starts. That last one was good, though, and a big improvement over her previous one, which was also run within the six-week requirement period.

Fresh Meadow does not have an index time. He is primarily a router, and while fast for these, we doubt if he can cope with the anticipated pace in this sprint. We expect he will "run out of track" before he gets his speed fully turned on.

Tocsin, then, is the only one left of our original speed horses which also has enough earn-ability-class ($892). He has had only one outing after being rested for three months but almost won at first asking. He was beaten only a neck on January 17 at Hialeah. But this race constitutes his best race in the index. And there are two others with better index time. South Point, (-13); and Candle Wood, (-10). South Point shot his bolt trying to match strides with Dark Ruler at Tropical on January 9. What Dark Ruler did to him is shown graphically in his next race in which he was unable to run fast enough to raise dust. We can't consider him at all. Candle Wood has been unable to regain his form since last October, though raced intermittently.

If we had entertained any idea of betting Tocsin, the betting action should have put an end to the thought, for he was bet down to 3/4 by the hungry fans. On our figures, he did not warrant such favoritism and was therefore a decided underlay. The fact that he won in a photo finish over Lady Elliott only strengthened our contention.

Tocsin paid $3.50, 2.60, and 2.40 across the board.

Before we leave this race, perhaps it is as good a place as any to make a point about how the racing secretary's conditions sometimes work to the disadvantage of some racers, and to the advantage of others. We have already mentioned that it is possible for an improving horse, one nearing peak and ready to win, to get in with a comparative feather under the conditions, while another that has passed his peak and is staling off may get the full treatment.

Tocsin, with high earn-ability and speed, the latter shown in an excellent effort only two weeks before (which didn't count against him because he didn't win), gets in with only 114 pounds, while such as Cosmonaut, Our Prince, and Singer, for instance, horses we discarded as unplayable anyway, had the heavy packages of 121, 123, and 123 respectively.

Under his light package, Tocsin was able to duplicate his (−8) peak form race, with five pounds less than he carried in making that best time.

It is well for the student to keep an eye open for these spots. Though Tocsin was not a healthy bet at such an underlay, there are times when a good betting tool is made better by this kind of unbalanced weight distribution.

SIXTH RACE

6 FURLONGS (Jet Action-Feb. 29,1956-1:09-5-120). **Purse,** $4,500. 4-year-olds and upward. Claiming. Weight, 126 lbs. Nonwinners since January 16 allowed 3 lbs.; December 10, 5 lbs.; November 20, 8 lbs. Claiming price, $12,000; 4 lbs. for each $1,000 to $10,000.

Another high-grade claimer at the six-furlong sprint distance. Here again, the initial selection is indicated as a speed problem with further separation by earn-ability.

The speed horses (our ratings) are: Vet's Boy, (−5½); Deep Breath, (−5¼); Viking Victory, (−5½); and Olympia Blend, (−3¼). (Ambers Folly, Woodbrook, Bomb Boo, Pie Bed, Admiral Vee, Two Fisted, Jutland, Helicopter, and Shooting Bull were scratched.)

Of these speed merchants, Vet's Boy gets an earn-ability-class of $680; Deep Breath, $835; Viking Victory, $497; and Olympia Blend, $675.

Olympia Blend is definitely staling off as per his speed line, $(-7\frac{3}{4})$-$(-6\frac{3}{4})$-$(-3\frac{1}{4})$. Viking Victory is racing way over his head. Not only is his earn-ability the lowest of the group, but a glance at his price line shows a sudden jump in claiming price in his last race of $10,000. Even at today's price of $12,000 he is still $5,000 over his best past race. His trainer must have been imbibing some heady stuff.

Deep Breath has had one outing at Hialeah, on January 23, after a rest of two months, and turns in a very respectable effort on a good (gd) track at today's distance. He ran fourth, but was not badly beaten and was closing steadily against $15,000 horses. His $(-5\frac{1}{4})$ speed rating off of this race is well below his peak ability which, from the index, is a (-14) from a 1:11⅗ effort on a *Slow* track (Mth). And he is getting the full eight-pound allowance under the conditions. There is, incidentally, a lot of speed noted in the index, of which Deep Breath's (-14) is five points the best. The second best, (-9) for Vet's Boy was made with a feather of 101 pounds, while he is carrying 115 today. And while we are on the subject of Vet's Boy and weight, let's look at an interesting situation which points up several statements we made earlier in the text.

In his second race back, Vet's Boy met I Geegee, and vanquished him at 5½ F. on a fast track. He carried 115 pounds while I Geegee carried 116.

Ten days later, the two meet again at 5½ F. and on a fast track, but this time I Geegee gets in with 107 pounds, a drop of nine pounds, while Vet's Boy again has 115. I Geegee beat him by 6½ lengths. That's one point we want to emphasize —the vanquished becoming the victor with a shift in weight. The other point is that so frequently a win, unless run in slower than index best time, takes too much off a horse's edge for him to come back soon with a comparable repeat performance. Vet's Boy had been all-out to beat I Geegee by a head (h), and ten days later, with the same weight, ran the same distance five points slower.

Today, in a desperate bid for another purse, his trainer puts him on the block at $10,000 in order to get eight pounds weight off. Hardly a recommendation.

Those wonderful people, the wagering fans, were looking the other way, and let Deep Breath get away at 3/1 while they were making Vet's Boy the favorite.

Even Ted Atkinson couldn't hold the staling Vet's Boy together. He finished fifth, beaten more than seven lengths by the improving Deep Breath, whose 1:10⅕ win earned him a (−9).

Deep Breath paid $8.00, 5.10, and 3.60 across the board.

SEVENTH RACE

This was the day's feature event at Hialeah and it presented a case of such outstanding class, in the person of Summer Tan, with ten stake races in his past performances and a per-race earn-ability of more than $20,000, that it was either a case of play Summer Tan or pass the race. The fact that he had not raced since November 22 at Pimlico meant little, for an expensive near-champ like this is never brought to the races unless he is in condition to win.

However, for the student to whom these things are not obvious, we will attempt to list his outstanding virtues, even though it seems superfluous to draw an analysis for this field. His earn-ability is three times as great as the next best, Nance's Lad. This alone is enough to elect him, for I have found this to be a rather lush win angle—just three times as much earn-ability-class as the next best one. But let's take it from scratch. the conditions:

7 FURLONGS (chute) (Crafty Admiral-Jan. 23, 1952-1:22-4-107) THE WINTER FESTIVAL. Purse, $7,500. 4-year-olds and upward, non-winners of three races since October 10 other than claiming. Allowances. Weight, 126 lbs. Non-winners of $10,000 twice in 1956 allowed 3 lbs.; $10,000 in 1956, or $4,500 three times in 1956, or $4,800 in 1957, 6 lbs.; $3,500 twice November 1, or a race since January 16, 9 lbs; two races October 10, 12 lbs.; a race, 15 lbs (claiming races not considered).

Maybe the racing secretary wasn't expecting Summer Tan to run for a $7,500 purse. Anyhow, he could have kept on giving weight away from here to yonder and he still couldn't have brought this band up even with Summer Tan.

Besides the extraordinary class superiority, he raced to a (−30) in his last race, which was 1¾₁₆ miles. But he won a HcpS, (a handicap stake) at Belmont at 7 furlongs which is today's distance. And he also won at 1⅝ miles. This, of course, is the mark of the champion, or near-champion, to be able to handle any distance and to lug weight.

Nance's Lad gets a (−11); I Appeal, (−11¼); Royal Briar, (−13½).

No, it just can't be done, fellers and gals. There's nothing in there that can match Summer Tan's (−30). The horse can take it in a breeze. He's an overlay at *any* price. He could also lose, but he'd just about have to drop dead to accomplish it.

EIGHTH RACE

1⅛ MILES (Spartan Valor-Feb. 9, 1952-1:47⅕-4-118) Purse, $4,000. Weight, 124 lbs. Non-winners twice since December 10 allowed 3 lbs.; a race, 6 lbs. Claiming price, $6,500.

This is just a plain old claimer, so we'll use our basic factor, earn-ability-class, to get the ball rolling. There are five of them worthy of analysis: Voyante, $543; Whence, $417; Returned Ring, $462; Activate, $866; and The Posse, $500.

Of these qualified contenders Voyante has much the best speed rating with a (-9); Whence, (-6); Returned Ring, (-5); Activate, (2); and The Posse, (1). Two others showed more speed, but we couldn't qualify them for other reasons. Armed Truce (-12) had per-race earn-ability of only $264, and had earned his index best time in his last race. His trainer has been running him over his head for some time.

Checkered Flag (-11), shows earn-ability of only $256, and is another one that has been running 'way over his head.

Activate, the high earn-ability hoss is an interesting case. He has a high-index of (-16) earned at Hialeah about a year ago, February, 1956. Something must have happened to him in this race, for, though he has had six races since, he has not been able to do better than a plus rating. It would seem as though after running his heart out on February 18, 1956, he has decided the hell with it.

I have seen other horses do the same thing. Two are especially fresh in my memory, though they ran some years ago. I was at Bay Meadows the day English Harry took a four-mile marathon by some 28 lengths against such seasoned marathoners as Bon Amour and Sweet Man. He got the bit in his teeth and made like a hoss in a hurry for the four full circuits of the track. He was sent out a few times after that but he had left his race on the track that day at Bay Meadows.

Challenge Me was the other one. He showed the best of them the way home at Santa Anita one day by many lengths, and never seemed to have much interest in racing after that.

To get back to Voyante, the second-high earn-ability and the highest speed rating of the qualified group of contenders. And he also has an excellent speed-line from the improvement standpoint: $-(6\frac{1}{2})-(0)-(-9)$. He has been improving by leaps and bounds. But won his last race, at $1\frac{1}{16}$. And that (-9) is 5 points faster than his best index time. This makes him doubtful for us, since we should not expect him to come right back and equal that good one. We would have to pass this one, reluctantly. But there is one other thing in his favor. His *present* class, per-race earn-ability off of his one outing in 1957, rates him at $1,550, which is more than three times as much as any other horse in the race shows for 1957. If we are flexible enough in our thinking, we could back Voyante with a clear conscience because of his better than 3 to 1 *present class*. It is the same sort of situation we had with Summer Tan, only to a lesser degree.

If your own personal analysis would let you go along with this, you might have tagged yourself a nice winner, for Voyante staved off Returned Ring's bold challenge and held on for a win that was worth $27.90, 9.30, and 5.20 across the board. He didn't run back to that (-9) of his last, $1\frac{1}{16}$ race, but he did turn in a (-5) which is one point better than his previous best time in the index. A truly improved horse, from this point of view. In any case, there are several object lessons here that account for the overlaid price. Those who gauge class by claiming price would feel Voyante was stepping up $1,500 after his winning effort, but you and I knew he was second only to Activate in overall class, and 3/1 the best in the race on present class. Others would say he was picking up five pounds off of that win and was therefore a bad betting medium. But you and I knew he had won with 119 and 120 pounds so that he was by no means overweighted. Such are some of the advantages of our flexible handicap-analysis.

NINTH RACE

The conditions for this race are exactly the same as for the eighth. Our high earn-ability horses were: In Clover, $695; Alan K., $770; Encono, $465; and Billy's Gem, $960. Of this group, In Clover had a speed rating of $(-\frac{1}{4})$; Alan K. (5); Encono, $(3\frac{1}{4})$; and Billy's Gem, (-9).

At first blush, Billy's Gem would seem to be the standout play, but don't let's ever jump to conclusions. Let's complete our analysis.

We find he's had two starts within the past six weeks. The one previous to the (−9) was a (−23) on a heavy track at today's distance. Actually, this exceeds the fast track, best time, shown in the index by 13 points, and it shows a decline of 14 points in that last race over the previous one. Also, Billy's Gem beat Stop Thief in that last race while the latter carried 118, and Billy's Gem lugged only 112. Both shoulder 121 today. And on the credit side for Billy's Gem is *present class* of $1,500 as against $644 for Encono and $525 for Icarian. This one had only $360 for over-all earn-ability.

So, Billy's Gem does not quite make it on the 3/1 better class than his next highest competition spot angle.

We look to Consistency for help. Billy's Gem won four fast track routes in six fast track tries, a win consistency of 67%. Encono was next best with 25%. This was the thing which tipped the balance in favor of a play instead of passing the race. And we got a run for our money, though we had to be satisfied with the show end of a photo finish. Icarian got the front money, and a 25/1 longshot named Galarch took the place by a head from Billy's Gem. Stop Thief was fourth.

Which only goes to prove that *nobody* wins them all, no matter how careful you try to be.

Following is a workout for the first six racing days (one week of racing) at Hialeah, February, 1957. It is, we believe, representative.

DATE	RACE	HORSE	WIN	PLACE	SHOW
2/1	1	Mark's Puzzle	$ 7.50	$ 4.20	$ 3.00
	2	Kismiss	. . .	10.90	5.50
	3	Edliss	5.20	3.50	2.60
	4	My Friend	. . .	4.90	3.90
	5	Tocsin	3.50	2.60	2.40

DATE	RACE	HORSE	WIN	PLACE	SHOW
	6	Deep Breath	8.00	5.10	3.60
	7	Summer Tan*	4.10	2.90	2.20
	8	Voyante	27.90	9.30	5.20
	9	Billy's Gem	. . .	. . .	3.60
2/2	1	Big Billie	22.10	12.70	8.60
	2	Moon Crazy	. . .	2.60	2.30
	3	Hoop Band	11.20	4.90	3.90
	4	Jodi	. . .	3.10	2.60
	5	Work Of Art	. . .	. . .	. . .
	6	Discernment	3.90	3.20	2.80
	7	Espea	12.50	5.90	4.20
	8	Chief Fanelli	. . .	. . .	. . .
	9	NO PLAY			
2/4	1	Gottapassem	. . .	8.80	5.50
	2	Baker Street	. . .	. . .	. . .
	3	NO PLAY			
	4	Nile Lily**	4.10	3.40	3.10
	5	Cagey Move	. . .	. . .	. . .
	6	Magic Spell	16.60	6.80	4.50
	7	Boy King	$94.30	$21.40	$10.40
	8	War Command	. . .	. . .	3.10
	9	NO PLAY			
2/5	1	NO PLAY			
	2	Googin	. . .	9.60	5.30
	3	Boycotter	6.70	3.80	3.40
4 & 5		NO PLAY			
	6	Lady Beaver	. . .	6.60	4.60
7 & 8		NO PLAY			
	9	Battle Talk	. . .	. . .	. . .
2/6	1	NO PLAY			
	2	Jedgar Ruler	11.40	3.60	3.00
	3	Sure Welcome	38.50	18.00	10.20
	4	Tachometer	. . .	. . .	4.10
	5	Captina	. . .	3.90	3.10
	6	Mince Pie	3.40	2.90	2.50
	7	Pucker Up	9.20	5.60	4.30
	8	One-Eyed-King	8.90	3.80	2.70
	9	Super Bug	. . .	. . .	. . .

DATE RACE HORSE		WIN	PLACE	SHOW
2/7	1 Go Between	. . .	3.80	2.90
	2 Discriminate**	34.40	11.90	8.50
	3-5 NO PLAY			
	6 Sky Master	11.30	5.40	3.30
	7 Light 'n Lovely	. . .	2.40	2.40
	8 First Served	. . .	5.80	4.10
	9 NO PLAY			

* At least 3 to 1 more class—spot play.
** Qualification came from rating workouts.

In the second race on February 7 of the workout, a six-furlong waltz for maiden fillies, we had a tie between Discriminate and Neshanic. Each had a plus six (6) for a speed rating off of his most recent race and neither had any earnings from which to delineate earn-ability-class. Here, we used the standards to rate recent workouts. From these we got a (-5) for Discriminate, and a (-2) for Neshanic. To qualify a horse off of workouts, do not use one done breezing (b). Either handily (h) or driving (d) can be used, and give preferential consideration to the longer workout distances.

We picked thirty-seven plays during the six days of this workout of which twenty-one won. This is nearly 57%, a good goal for you to shoot at. And there's no reason you cannot do as well, once you have gained the necessary facility and flexibility through practice. However, handicap-analysis must necessarily be a personal thing, so results will vary according to the individual. For this reason, there would be little point in supplying a longer workout. The student-fan should find most situations for comparison in the week given. In system play, on the other hand, where rules are hard and fast, each selector should get substantially the same results.

Now then, before we leave the chapter on handicap-analysis, we want to take a look at the results for Sunshine Park for a similar period of time. This is important. I could hardly supply you with better proof of the soundness of this flexible handicap-analysis procedure, for, as I mentioned earlier, Hialeah and Sunshine Park are the Hi and Lo of Florida winter racing. This is meant as no reflection on Sunshine Park. It is showing good improvement every year, and in the forseeable future will doubtless come into its own. For the present, I am happy to be able to present such a wide divergence of competition for your comparison and edification.

In making this second workout, I have followed essentially the same general procedure with perhaps slightly more stress on the speed factor since earn-ability-class is virtually nonexistent in some of these contests. For that matter, we do not see very many minus speed ratings at SP, either, which substantiates my claim that speed and class *are* complimentary.

There were twenty-eight plays during the six days selected for. Seventeen of them won. This is 60%, slightly higher than our percentage at Hialeah, though we did a little better on price at the more illustrious oval. Here they are:

DATE	RACE	HORSE	WIN	PLACE	SHOW
2/1	1	Melody Air	$ 3.50	$ 2.80	$ 2.70 (Underlay)
	2	Deflation	6.30	4.30	5.30
	3	Hearts Buzz	3.70	2.40	2.40
	4	NO PLAY			
	5	Sure Time	10.90	4.50	2.70
	6	NO PLAY			
	7	Wedding Ring	15.80	7.10	4.90
	8	NO PLAY			
	9	Proscenium	7.60	3.80	3.60
2/2	1	NO PLAY (Sergeant Spook underlaid @ 3 to 5)			
	2	Sir Pick	. . .	. . .	. . .
	3	Rissa's Son	7.60	3.80	3.60
	4	Rip Luck	. . .	3.50	3.10
	5-6	NO PLAY			
	7	Bleak	. . .	. . .	. . .
	8	Bob o' Nick	. . .	. . .	. . .

DATE	RACE	HORSE	WIN	PLACE	SHOW
	9	Birmooda	12.90	8.10	4.80
2/4	1	NO PLAY			
	2	Beach Party	. . .	. . .	3.00
	3	Mozzell	5.10	3.70	3.40
	4	Jofin	. . .	. . .	2.60
	5-6	NO PLAY			
	7	Monsieur Tiger	10.40	5.80	7.10
	8-9	NO PLAY			
2/5	1	NO PLAY			
	2	We Depend	$12.10	$ 5.40	$ 4.70
	3	Ydidweleave	8.10	5.00	3.50
	5	NO PLAY			
	6	Hunch Play	8.40	2.90	2.60
	7-8-9	NO PLAY			
2/6	1-2	NO PLAY			
	3	King Of Kings	. . .	4.10	2.70
	4	NO PLAY-Underlay			
	5	Driving	. . .	4.00	3.80
	6-7-8-9	NO PLAY			
2/7	1	NO PLAY			
	2	Sergeant Spook	5.20	4.10	3.40
	3	Anita's Folly	. . .	. . .	. . .
	4	Kate's Rebel	4.40	2.90	2.50
	5	Millcamp	8.50	4.70	3.10
	6-7	NO PLAY			
	8	Harry Husman	5.20	3.00	3.00
	9	Son Al	. . .	. . .	. . .

NOTE: Those of you who use the Miami edition of the *Form* to check this will see no index given in the SP past performances. Therefore, you will have to gauge improvement and best previous speed entirely from past performances shown.

11. Profit Gobblers

Before we get involved with system play, it might be well to spend a short chapter discussing what I call "Profit Gobblers." These are the superstitions, suspicions, instabilities in our emotional get-up or temperament, and the various foibles through which the hoss player delivers himself into one blind switch after another.

Let's haul some of these out in the open, so that we may see how senseless they are and can thus dispel them from among our idiosyncrasies. Forewarned is forearmed, or so the saying goes.

Aside from the everyday brand of superstition like the black cat, number 13, or walking under ladders, there are some peculiar to the race track which, if allowed to affect our judgement, can and will cost us money.

For instance, there is a widespread belief around the tracks among the unthinking, that post position number one is disadvantageous. This I call a superstition because it has no basis in fact. The argument is, of course, that the rest of the field will crowd the number-one horse over into the rail. This disregards the fact that close to the rail is the shortest way home, and all jocks are required to hold their mounts straight until there is sufficient room to cross over. A jock disregarding this safety rule will quickly find himself in trouble with the stewards. Even if crowding were allowed, a fast-breaking horse would still have a big advantage breaking from the number-one post.

A breakdown of winning posts will prove to you conclusively that the number-one post produces its share of winners —far more, in fact, than the outside posts, where the horse is free of the alleged crowding into the rail. Even a fast-breaking horse, breaking from an outside post position, must give away valuable lengths to cross over to the rail. Or he might not be able to get over and therefore would be forced to race the entire distance via the "overland trail." Many a race has been lost right at the start by a jockey forcing his mount to extend himself in the early stages to get over on the rail on top or at least in contention, and thus having nothing left when the real test comes in the stretch run. If the rail is so bad, why do all jocks try so hard to get there?

Have you heard the one about white horses never winning? And if so, how many white thoroughbreds have you ever seen on any man's track? That's right, they're rare indeed. But this doesn't stop the superstitious. Lacking white horses to blame, he enlarges the superstition to include gray horses, and that is just plain ridiculous. Take a look at the record book of important stakes winners. The grays are well represented. Remember Native Dancer?

And what about these superstitious birds who get all in a tizzy if the parimutuel clerk from whom they buy a ticket is thoughtless enough to say "Thank you." Yeah man. That's supposed to be awfully bad luck. How silly can they get? Since when has it been unlucky to be courteous—even at a madhouse like the average hoss track where most of the cash customers seem to make a habit of leaving their manners outside the gate?

If you have done your work well, and your figures and your judgment indicate a certain beastie, play him no matter what his post position, and no matter what color his hide is, and no matter if the mutuel clerk sends you an engraved "thank you" note. Forget superstition. Stick to facts and figures.

I think that the suspicious player is even worse off than the superstitious one. He is suspicious of everyone, the owner, the trainer, the guinea, the jockey, the stewards and the track management. They're all watching him to see which horse he bets on and then all get together in a grand slam conspiracy to defeat this one poor lone two-buck operator. Of course, this guy's suspicion is a cover-up for his own ineptitude as a selector.

Leg bandages: These do not indicate that a horse is dickey-legged. If he had to be patched up to get him to the post, he'd never get by the track veterinarian. Some horses, when running all out, will clip themselves on the ankles with their flying hoofs. Small cuts and bruises result which can be costly and time-consuming in healing. The bandages prevent these horses from hurting themselves. Yet the uninformed and the suspicious will pass up a bandaged horse no matter if he's the obvious choice. This would be all right if they passed the race altogether. I have no quarrel with a fan for passing a race where a doubt exists in his mind. In fact, I recommend it. But these birds who shy away from leg bandages usually pass up only the bandaged horse, not the race. They'll go to something else, and they never seem to remember how many times that hoss in the bandages beat them.

Few businesses are subject to such rigid controls as is horse racing. Few businesses are as honestly run. If we have the kind of nature that must be suspicious of somebody or something, let's save it for the neighbor's wife, or the politicians, and keep our mind clear and open where making an honest buck is the end point.

Have you ever seen Blind-switch Benny in operation? Without bothering to read the conditions, Benny will arbitrarily decide consistency is the answer. So he is beaten by the speed merchant. In the next he goes to the speed horse, naturally, and is beaten by the class horse. So he goes to the class horse, though obviously out of form, and is beaten by the consistent cheapie. He never gets off the merry-go-round. When Benny does get hold of a good one, he can be touted off by anybody, and we do mean *anybody*. Or if nobody happens to be interested in touting him at the moment, he can get himself off on a tangent by a glance at the tote board. Either the odds are too high or too low. So, standing in line at the parimutuel window, Benny absorbs the various opinions of the assorted Saturday afternoon handicappers and changes his mind a half dozen times. Then the bird in front of him bets and he just catches the number, for the guy asks for his ticket in a half-whispered, conspiratorial voice. Obviously he is on the inside of an important manipulation. Benny goes along, for Benny is a screwball. And he's caught in another blind switch.

That tote board is not one of these electronic brains, capable of supplying the answer before the race, and all those master manipulators who comprise the wagering public do not—believe me—know which end of a horse eats. You already know a helluva lot more than they do, because you've read this far, and if you'll do your work the best you can and stick to your pre-decided plan of operation, you're well on your way to becoming one of the chosen few. But the moment you let superstition, suspicion, or blind-switchitis rule your play, Benny will move over and make room for you on the merry-go-round.

There is one more profit gobbler which takes a heavy toll of winnings. This is lack of confidence. The selector who has to compare his findings with the pix of the public handicappers has no confidence in himself or his method. He might just as well not waste the time selecting, but accept the public selectors' pix and take his beating. What other possible reason could a person have for learning to make his own selections if it is not the hope of out-picking the so-called experts? Since we know the public selectors and the bet favorites are sure roads to financial insolvency, why should we check our work against either the expert or the tote board, unless, in the latter case, we are using a strictly tote board method, such as playing even-money or odds-on favorites to place or show and compare our findings to avoid play on the public's false favorites?

If you can't feel real confidence in your method and/or your own ability, then by all means use one of the systems which we will present in the following pages. They will supply your action without any handicapping on your part whatsoever. Even with these, you must check sufficiently to gain confidence. Without it, you're licked.

12. The Hit and Run System

By way of a change of pace, and a rest from the labors of handicapping, the first system offered is for those patient souls who have been waiting for me to fulfill my promise that they can beat the races without doing a lick of handicapping. Some fans simply do not have analytical minds and therefore need something direct and entirely mechanical in order to persuade the parimutuel monster to cough up a bob or two.

For the Hit and Run System, all the fan needs in the way of equipment is a pencil and some scratch paper or a note book, and the small ability to do some simple mathematics. And, of course, when he has checked it and gained sufficient confidence to take it to the racing wars, a bit of operating capital.

This system I conceived and tested under fire during the 1956 season in Florida, so I will use the original workout to substantiate my claims for it.

The plays will be taken directly from the tote board about five minutes before post time, to allow the operator enough time to do some quick figuring and then transact his business at the parimutuel windows.

We will play two (2) horses, both of them to win, and both of them quoted as near to 3/1 as possible, but not less than three to one. The reason for this limiting of odds is to avoid a too-high operating capital. The amounts bet on each of these hides will depend on the odds at the time of play. This, in turn, is regulated by our pre-conceived idea of how much cash profit we want to take home—our day's hoss track wages, if you will.

Supposing we decide we want to take home a double sawbuck. Twenty dollars is a nice round figure. And let's suppose Horse A on the tote is quoted right at 3/1, which means a payoff, if he wins, of approximately $8.00 plus some odd change. In order to take home a net of at least $20, we must wager enough on this three-to-one shot to assure the return of our investment on both this one and the second horse we will play. So, suppose the second horse is shown at 5/1. We would have to play four tickets ($8.00) on Horse A, which would bring a minimum return of $32 if he gets home free. On Horse B, at 5/1, which means a $12.00 minimum pay-off if successful, we would have to invest $6.00 for three win tickets. This would provide us with a gross return of $36.00 in the event he was the winner.

So, in this example, we would have a total investment of $14.00 ($8 on Horse A, and $6 on Horse B). If Horse A wins and pays exactly $8.00 (he'd probably pay something more than that) our return would be the minimum anticipated ($32.00) and after subtracting our investment of $14.00 we would have $18.00 net to take home. If Horse B wins, the investment subtracted from minimum anticipated return would leave a net of $22.00.

If neither of them wins, we repeat the same procedure in the next race, only this time we must invest enough to pick up our $14 loss in the first race, plus our investment in this race, plus our $20 take-home pay. In other words, the net profit in this race will have to be $34 ($14 plus $20). If this one hits, we run for home. Or at least stop play for the day. No matter if you hit in the very first race, and you will quite frequently, the day's action is over as soon as you have your take home pay in your pocket.

This is important, for by quitting as soon as you get your winner, you will be able to maintain a very high win percentage. If you were to start a new series of action endlessly, carrying over any unfinished business to the following day, you would pull your win percentage way down and put a considerable strain on your operating capital, and on your nervous system. I cannot recommend that you play this any other way than hit and run. If you want more take home pay, step up the size of your requirements and *stop* as soon as you get your winner each day. This is just another way of getting the percentages working with you.

It is true that there will be times when this would hit three or four times during one afternoon. There will be other times when it may hit only once all afternoon. Play for that one win, and go home happy every racing day.

Let's take a couple of plays in the actual workout and work them through step by step to make sure the procedure is understood.

In the first race on February 2, 1956, there was no horse quoted at 3/1. The nearest was Time For Fun at 4/1 and the second selection was Hurbane at 5/1. So 4/1 equals an anticipated (minimum) payoff of $10.00. Three tickets would give a return of $30.00. This is an investment of $6.00. Hurbane would require the same bet as two tickets would give promise of only a $24 return. Of course, we could get a five-dollar pasteboard on Hurbane if we had time, but we only started to function five minutes before post time, remember, and we nearly have to plan to get all our tickets in one line to avoid getting shut out.

Anyhow, in this particular case, neither of them had his mind on his business, so we take our play into the second race with a deficit of $12.00.

At five minutes before post time, Bob O Boy is 3/1 on the tote board, and Raggylug is 7/2, which is 3½ to 1 for the uninitiated. Since 3/1 is an anticipated payoff of $8, and 7/2 is $9, and since we have to clear $32.00 to earn our take home pay, we are going to have to have 8 two buck ducats on each. $32 to pick up and $32 invested in this race means we have to gross $64. The eight tickets on Bob O Boy at an anticipated $8 payoff equals $64, and the eight tickets on Raggylug promise a minimum payoff of $72. No, that's more than we need, so we'll change our bet on Raggylug to seven tickets. This makes our necessary gross $62. Seven tickets times $9 equals $63, so now we have it.

Always keep capital investment down to rock bottom needed to come out because we never know in advance just how far we will have to go before a hit, and if we play too much on losers, the required eventual capital for a hit will be correspondingly higher.

By the time we got back from buying our tickets, the odds on Bob O Boy had dropped to 5/2, and since it's too late to do anything about it anyway, we'll let the thing ride the way it is. After all, even a seven-buck payoff will clear $56, which would leave us a take-home pay of $14, and the next time our odds will go up after we buy and make us more than we anticipated. I tell you this so you won't worry if you occasionally get an odds drop after buying.

So Bob O Boy won this one, and when the payoff was posted, we got $7.90, just 10¢ under 3/1, making our gross $63.20. Now since our total investment, $12 from the first race and $30 in the second, stands us $42, we have a take-home pay of $21.20. Time to go home.

The real test of this system is whether the fan will have fortitude enough to quit when he has his profit. If he is strong minded, he might want to stay and watch the balance of the card, and the antics of the two-buck improvers of the breed trying to run a deuce into a million. If he is not strong willed, he'd better run for home.

In the first race on February 2nd, Flip's Joy at 4/1 and Speedy Van at 7/1 were our standard bearers for a total investment of $10. ($6 on the 4/1 shot and $4 on the 7/1 shot.) Neither won.

In the second race, Quarterwave at 4/1, and Kid Brown at 9/1 were our two plays, and the investment was $12 on Quarterwave and $6 on Kid Brown. Again we drew a blank. We are now involved for $28, which means we'll have to clear a net of $48 to make the take home pay we promised ourselves.

In the third race the tote board gives us Nile Prince at 7/2 and Halara at 5/1, and bets of $18 and $14 respectively. And we blew this one, too. So now we're in the soup for $60, going into the fourth.

Here we find both Treadmill and Bow Buttons being quoted at 3/1 about five minutes before post time. We have to invest $40 each on these two for a total of $80. We anticipate a gross of $160 minimum if either wins. We have a total of $140 involved. Treadmill turned back his competition, and the payoff was $8.20. Gross, $164. Take-home, $24. We go home.

We'll do one more day, and by then even the very new fan should be able to follow through.

Russett, in the first race on February 3, was quoted at 3/1 about five minutes before post time, and Gal Proof at 7/2. We can anticipate a minimum payoff of $8.00 on Russett, and $9.00 of Gal Proof. By now, a quick glance should tell us we're going to have to get a gross of forty dollars to pay back our investment and leave us with $20 take-home pay. Five two-buck tickets on Russett (or two fives, or one ten) will gross forty. And we'll have to buy the same on Gal Proof, which will gross a minimum of $45. If there were plenty of time, a nine-dollar investment would do the trick—one five and two twos. Let's say that in the interest of keeping our investment at a minimum at all times, we'll take the time to buy at the two different windows, and thus the race gets under way with us holding ten bucks on Russett and nine on Gal Proof.

Here again we find the odds have dropped on one of our horses while we were at the wagering stalls. Russett is now shown at 5/2. We don't care.

Russett showed them all the way home, and the official payoff was $7.90. This is a gross (for five tickets) of $39.50. Investment, $19. Take-home, $20.50.

Take a look at the month's work which follows.

WORKOUT

NOTE: Each succeeding MINUS column figure includes previous minus figure plus investment in subject race.

Sunshine Park   *February, 1956*

DATE	RACE	HORSE	ODDS	BET	MUTUEL	MINUS	PLUS
2/1	1	Time For Fun	4/1	$ 6			
	1	Hurbane	5/1	4		$ 10	
	2	Bob O Boy	3/1	16	$ 7.90		
	2	Raggylug	7/2	14			$21.20
2/2	1	Flip's Joy	4/1	6			
	1	Speedy Van	7/1	4		10	
	2	Quarterwave	4/1	12			
	2	Kid Brown	9/1	6		28	
	3	Nile Prince	7/2	18			
	3	Halara	5/1	14		60	
	4	Treadmill	3/1	40	8.20		
	4	Bow Buttons	3/1	40			$24.00
2/3	1	Russett	3/1	10	7.90		
	1	Gal Proof	7/2	9			$20.50
2/4	1	Clouded Sun	3/1	10			
	1	Lady Cowboy	9/2	8		18	
	2	Falstaff	9/2	12			
	2	Hab	8/1	6		36	
	3	Treadmill	6/1	12			
	3	Big Trick	6/1	12		60	
	4	Kin Trip	7/2	28	9.10		
	4	Ann-Mar	8/1	14			$25.40

DATE	RACE	HORSE	ODDS	BET	MUTUEL	MINUS	PLUS
2/6	1	Jackie Pet	4/1	$ 6			
	1	Margaret M.	4/1	6		$ 12	
	2	Flip's Joy	3/1	16			
	2	Arthur Charles	5/1	11		39	
	3	Roy Prince	3/1	34			
	3	Light Dawn	9/2	24	$11.90	00	$27.80
2/7	1	Cribbage	3/1	8			
	1	Minsi	9/2	6		14	
	2	Time For Fun	5/1	8			
	2	Time Honored	11/1	5		27	
	3	Grey Granite	5/1	16	12.40		
	3	McBezzill	6/1	10		00	$24.20
2/8	1	Secret Passion	7/2	8			
	1	Nell Keegan	6/1	5		13	
	2	Nile Prince	7/2	14			
	2	Light Dawn	7/2	14	9.50	00	$25.50
2/9	1	Zaca Prize	3/1	10	8.20		
	2	Gareth	3/1	10		00	$21.00
2/10	1	Clouded Sun	5/1	5			
	1	Cock Fight	5/1	5		10	
	2	Sugar Ham	4/1	8			
	2	Gene's Bid	12/1	4		22	
	3	Bean Beau	3/1	18			
	3	Sun Crisp	5/1	12		52	
	4	King's Blood	7/2	$ 28			
	4	Star Show	4/1	26	$10.00	$ 00	$24.00
2/11	1	Yellow House	7/1	4			
	1	Never Better	5/1	5		9	
	2	I Tolya So	3/1	12			
	2	Deeside	7/1	6		27	
	3	Solero Jr.	3/1	22			
	3	Gray Vision	4/1	18		67	
	4	Little Bandit	9/2	22			
	4	Henry D.M.	9/1	12	20.70	00	$23.20
2/13	1	Cross End	3/1	10	8.70		
	1	Platterette	3/1	10		00	$23.50
2/14	1	Little Gig	5/1	5	13.80		
	1	Cranberry	5/1	5		00	$24.50

DATE	RACE	HORSE	ODDS	BET	MUTUEL	MINUS	PLUS
2/15	1	Hypostyle	3/1	10			
	1	Clouded Sun	7/2	9	9.70	00	*$24.65*
2/16	1	Destino's Date	7/2	8			
	1	Where Now	4/1	7		15	
	2	Sagmate	3/1	16			
	2	Jet Blue Bird	4/1	12		43 (Wo.-Dis.)	
	3	Wynne's Due	4/1	20			
	3	Miss Allright	9/2	18		81	
	4	Col. Hardboot	7/2	28			
	4	Gray Vision	8/1	14		123	
	5	Oalo	7/2	$ 48			
	5	Very Stylish	4/1	44		$215	
	6	Turkey Boots	4/1	68			
	6	Bobby's Bull	7/1	42		345	
	7	Daring Spirit	4/1	130	$10.30		
	7	Cant O'Mar	4/1	130		00	*$25.00*
2/17	1	Flip's Joy	3/1	10	$ 8.40		
	1	Changeaway	7/2	9		00	*$23.00*
2/18	1	Sugar Ham	4/1	7			
	1	Mr. Pan	4/1	7		14	
	2	Ari's Brig	5/1	8			
	2	Ari's Brig	5/1	8		30	
	3	Whirltown	9/2	14			
	3	Flaneur	6/1	10		54	
	4	Memaw	4/1	24			
	4	Old Booty	5/1	20		98	
	5	Bob O Boy	4/1	38			
	5	Go Go Go	4/1	38		174	
	6	Long Lick	3/1	80			
	6	Henry D.M.	9/2	58		312	
	7	D'Arbonne	3/1	136			
	7	Put Out	7/2	120		568	
	8	Night Baker	6/1	178	$14.30		
	8	Rebut	7/1	154		00	*$31.00*
2/20	1	Cherry Stone	6/1	$ 4			
	1	Stewy	6/1	4		$ 8	
	2	Valley Sprite	3/1	11			
	2	Changeaway	5/1	7	$13.60	00	*$21.60*

DATE	RACE	HORSE	ODDS	BET	MUTUEL	MINUS	PLUS
2/21	1	Cock Fight	3/1	8			
	1	Bayou Waif	4/1	7		15	
	2	Challcote	5/1	9			
	2	Atone	6/1	8		32	
	3	Reine Lea	7/2	18			
	3	Plain Jim	5/1	14		64	
	4	Shooting Box	7/2	28			
	4	Mattafor	7/2	28		120	
	5	Juke	3/1	56			
	5	Cash Request	6/1	34		210	
	6	Clouded Sun	7/2	80			
	6	Oalo	4/1	72	$10.00	00	*$25.20*
2/22	1	Chance Tip	5/1	5			
	1	Treadmill	8/1	4		9	
	2	Lady Cowboy	3/1	14			
	2	Lysbeth	6/1	8	$15.90	00	*$32.60*
2/23	1	Sugar Ham	3/1	9	$ 8.90		
	1	Sagmate	5/1	6		00	*$22.00*
2/24	1	Range Cardinal	7/2	8			
	1	Ari's Brig	5/1	6	$13.00	00	*$25.00*
2/25	1	Reine Lea	6/1	$ 4			
	1	Whirltown	7/1	4		$ 8	
	2	Black Al	9/2	8			
	2	Trenton Sand	5/1	7		23	
	3	Green Cross	4/1	14	$10.10		
	3	Clouded Sun	6/1	10		00	*$23.70*
2/27	1	Nell Keegan	6/1	4			
	1	Heureux	8/1	4		8	
	2	Hypostyle	3/1	12			
	2	Mahatma II	9/2	9		29	
	3	Treadmill	3/1	20			
	3	Miss Allright	9/1	8		57	
	4	Brentwoodian	5/1	18			
	4	Foxie Flag	13/1	8	$29.10	00	*$23.40*
2/28	1	Dr. Ci	7/2	8			
	1	Jake's Julep	5/1	6		14	
	2	Destino's Date	5/1	10			
	2	Do Bee Tee	3/1	16		40	

DATE	RACE	HORSE	ODDS	BET	MUTUEL	MINUS	PLUS
	3	Tad's Pursuit	4/1	20			
	3	Bim's Gem	9/1	10		70	
	4	Jahar	6/1	18	$15.00		
	4	North Steed	8/1	14		00	*$33.00*
2/29	1	Rival Time	4/1	7	$10.20		
	1	Nell Keegan	4/1	7		00	*$21.70*

Now let's break this workout down and see what we've got. First off, you'll want to know how much profit there was. Our net was $616.65 for a yield of 22% on total invested capital.

We played a total of seventy-one races and won twenty-five of them. This is 35.2%, or some 3% *higher* than the annual average for bet favorites. But our average mutuel was $11.62 as against less than six dollars average for the bet favorites.

It will be noted that we had a couple of sustained runs, one on February 16 taking us through seven races and another on February 18 taking us through eight races. If you think these might be too rough on your nervous system, and available bankroll, you can make it a rule never to play beyond the fourth race on any one day. If you fail to hit in four races, go home and continue the play with the first race the next day. In this way, for instance, that seven-race run would have been resolved in five (four races on 2/16 and one 2/17. Or the eight-race run would have been broken in six (four races on 2/18 and the first and second races on the following day).

If this plan had been adhered to, the net profit would have been about fifty dollars less, but nearly six hundred dollars less capital would have been needed to clear the longest one.

So here we have a solid system which can be operated profitably by a novice without any handicapping knowledge whatsoever. He can walk into any track in the country and commence operating without any preparation whatsoever. And he'll know within a buck or so exactly what his day's profit will be.

13. Mud

The "off" track—good (gd); sloppy (sy); slow (sl); muddy (m); and heavy (hy)—immediately creates a mental hazard for many unenlightened fans and some experienced speculators. This is understandable, as a lot of hogwash has been written about so-called "mudders" which has given the mistaken general feeling that in order to win on an "off" track, we must have a speaking acquaintance with only those animals that are part duck and/or 100% pig.

'T'ain't so, fellers and gals, 't'ain't so.

The answer to successful operation in the goo is the same as for successful operation on a fast track. *Peak present form.*

By this I do not mean that some horses do not "step up" in the "off" going. Definitely they do. But they are comparatively rare and are not going to upset the apple cart often enough to alter our averages appreciably. And even these so-called superior mudders have to be at or very near peak in order to give a good account of themselves.

As for the mud marks in the *Form* or *Telegraph*, they are utterly meaningless unless the hoss in question is sharp as hands can make him. On the other hand, a beastie with nary a sign of mud mark, and without an indication that he has been "bred for mud," can sail through the goo like a true mudlark if he enjoys a razor-sharp edge at the time he is asked the question.

By the same token, that there are a few outstanding mudders, there are a few, also, that will simply not extend themselves on any but a fast track. But by and large, the horse that figures as the class and speed of a given race, is a reliable betting tool on any kind of track if he is at peak or approaching peak by our tests.

The sharp horse, then, who also shows a good past record in the muck, is a good betting medium for us when the footing is "off." By the same analysis, if his "off" track races look bad, and we can convince ourselves he *was in condition* at the time, then we can be sure he is one of the ones that flattens out in the goo. On the other hand, if he was not in top form at the time of those bad mud races, they don't mean a thing—except that he was off-form.

A simple way to pick your contenders, if you are a user of the New York *Telegraph,* when the track is off, or drying out, or wholly returned to fast but most contestants are still showing their most recent efforts in the soup, is to add together the last three speed ratings without regard to track condition, then add together the last three variants and lump the whole thing into one grand total. The eventual winner will be the one of the higher lumped numbers which also shows sharp present condition, such as a strong closing effort in his last race or an in-the-money performance in the same—close-up, of course. Or better yet, our speed-line pattern of improvement which is approaching index best time.

The mere fact that so many players are jumpy and uncertain when the track is "off", makes for some whopping big overlays to be taken by the selector with the know-how.

For instance, look at February 2 of the handicap-analysis workout at Hialeah. We hit three winners out of seven tries, one of which was for ninety-four dollars. The track was *slow* this day.

Track condition was at no time taken into consideration for the workout in Chapter 12, nor for the earn-ability workout in Chapter 4.

The editor of one of the better turf magazines once asked me if I would develop an "off" track system for his readers. I couldn't do it. There is no such animal, unless you could call most any sound fast track method with particular attention to whether or not the animal flattened out in previous races when he was in peak form, an "off" track system. Actually, it is an "off" track system just as much as it is a fast track system.

So let's discard the "off" track bugaboo in the same worry basket with superstition and suspicion. The fastest and classiest hoss, in top form, is the one for our money.

14. The Chronology System

We mentioned earlier in the text that chronology is important to the workability of a system and to the results obtained from more or less systematic handicap-analysis procedure. In the latter case, the analyst will determine his chronology for each race after a study of the racing secretary's conditions. Thus the burden of deciding the chronological use of the factors is part and parcel of the analysis.

For the system player, the burden must be shifted to the system itself, for the chief virtue of any system is the short-cuts it offers and the substitution of rules for the unwanted pressures of personal judgement.

If the analyst gets the cart before the horse on occasion, he may lose a race, but a system player may lose his shirt if the system he is using has the factors in the wrong chronological order. Dissimilar results can be obtained by reversing the chronological order of the use of the handicapping factors.

To point up this difference, we are now going to base a system on speed and class, and supply a one-month workout of the results. Then we will reverse the chronology of these two basic and complimentary factors to produce an entirely different set of results. We can assure you the revelation will be rather startling.

In the first workout, speed will be used to isolate the group of contenders from which the eventual winner should emerge. Class will then be used as the factor to point up which of these contenders should ring the bell.

To avoid putting too much work on the system player, and to supply some of the flexibility we promised earlier, we will side-step our own method of speed determination, even though we consider it superior, and avail ourselves of the ready-made speed ratings in the *Form* or *Telegraph*.

Where possible, we will take these ratings for a fast track effort at today's distance. However, since the majority of races will not supply us with a race for each contestant at exactly today's distance on a fast track, we will call on flexibility to get us past this hurdle.

Where a contestant does not have a race at exactly today's distance on a fast track, we will accept the closest thing to it. So, if today's race is carded at a sprint distance, we will accept the contestant's most recent race, in his past performances, at a sprint distance provided it was run on a fast track. Likewise, if today's distance is a route (over a mile) we will accept, where necessary, a route speed rating over a fast track.

Our contenders, then, will be the group which falls within the limits of five speed points. For instance, if the highest speed rating in the race is 90, then we will accept all those horses as contenders with speed ratings between 85-90. Anything below 85 will be discarded as too slow for this band. Thus the system-student can reduce the field to an easily workable minimum (the number will vary from race to race, but will average about five) quickly, easily, and with reasonable accuracy, though it must be understood that our comparable speed standards are better if the system player is willing to indulge in the extra work.

Now, to this group of contenders, we apply the class factor

to point up the one worthy of carrying our wager. Class will be on the basis of earn-ability. By using a slide rule to make the division of number of starts into money earned, we have the fastest, most accurate, and most work-free class delineation we know of.

Our play, then, will be the one of the group already separated on a speed basis which now shows the highest per-race earn-ability. He may not be the highest earn-ability in the race, but he will be the highest among the pre-selected contenders. And for the purpose of this system, let us say that $300 will be the minimum earn-ability we will consider as indicative of significant class on the better ovals, at least. At the cheaper tracks we would have to call on our flexibility and adjust this minimum downward enough to give us the amount of action necessary to keep us happy. Depending on the grade of track, we might have to adjust downward to a $200 minimum. Or $100. But for this workout, which is Hialeah during February of 1956, we hold the minimum to $300. So those races not selected for in the workout, either showed insufficient earn-ability, or were unseparated ties.

WORKOUT #1
(Before reversing for Chronology)

Hialeah   *February, 1956*

DATE	RACE	HORSE	WIN	PLACE	SHOW
2/1	1	Beguile	$ . . .	$ . . .	$3.10
	2	Whittledy Cut	4.30	3.30	2.60
	3	Hoptoitboy	4.10	2.90	2.40
	4	Cedar Jungle	. . .	. . .	. . .
	5	Squared Away	4.60	3.70	3.00
	6	Tollesboro	. . .	2.50	2.30
	7	Dark Charger	. . .	10.80	8.10
	8	Happy New Year	. . .	. . .	. . .
	9	Topside	7.40	4.10	3.50
2/2	1	Shining Star	. . .	. . .	. . .
	2	Tombouctou	. . .	. . .	. . .

DATE	RACE	HORSE	WIN	PLACE	SHOW
	4	Overland	. . .	. . .	. . .
	5	Acclivity	. . .	. . .	. . .
	6	Bless Pat	. . .	3.20	2.70
	7	Queen Hopeful	. . .	4.50	3.10
	8	Skeptical Kid	. . .	. . .	. . .
	9	Winning Fleet	. . .	. . .	. . .
2/3	2	War Age	4.70	3.30	2.70
	3	Gottemnow	9.10	5.00	4.20
	4	Top-Lation	. . .	. . .	. . .
	5	Auratum	. . .	. . .	. . .
	6	Black Record	3.40	2.70	2.20
	7	First Cadet	. . .	. . .	. . .
	8	Craigwood	$ . . .	$ . . .	$3.40
	9	Sea Tale	. . .	7.90	4.50
2/4	1	Assistance	. . .	3.70	2.80
	2	Grey Falcon	. . .	. . .	3.10
	3	Java Belle	. . .	3.10	2.60
	4	Stevies Pal	. . .	. . .	. . .
	5	Music Maestro	16.10	7.20	5.70
	6	Helfast	. . .	. . .	. . .
	7	Monk Shoe	. . .	. . .	. . .
	8	Diving Board	. . .	. . .	. . .
	9	Oclirock	7.20	4.20	3.70
2/6	1	Socko	. . .	3.70	2.90
	2	College Chum	. . .	. . .	. . .
	3	Mr. Blue Sky	. . .	. . .	4.10
	4	Cascanuez	3.90	3.40	3.00
	5	Doc Walker	6.00	4.20	2.80
	6	Fabulous Fox	. . .	. . .	2.20
	7	Nail	. . .	. . .	. . .
	8	Kope's Baby (e) *	12.10	10.10	6.00
	9	Retarmo	. . .	. . .	. . .
2/7	1	Crann	. . .	. . .	. . .
	2	Dun Dandy	. . .	. . .	. . .
	5	Beautillion	5.00	3.30	2.50
	6	Sometime Thing	3.70	2.30	2.20
	7	Lawless	$ 6.30	$ 4.30	$3.20
	8	Ankara	. . .	. . .	5.50

DATE	RACE	HORSE	WIN	PLACE	SHOW
	9	Go Between	11.50	6.40	5.10
2/8	1	Pasha Saied	5.00	3.30	2.70
	2	Steps Babe	. . .	. . .	7.90
	4	Wagon Drill	16.10	4.60	3.60
	5	Hickory Hill	. . .	. . .	3.60
	6	Dark Ruler	. . .	2.90	2.40
	7	Tiswar	. . .	. . .	. . .
	8	Commodore M.	. . .	3.70	2.50
	9	Gallant Fanar	. . .	. . .	. . .
2/9	1	Yoeman	12.70	8.00	5.10
	2	Seebit	. . .	. . .	. . .
	4	Teri	. . .	. . .	4.30
	5	McKean's Gold	. . .	. . .	. . .
	6	P.O.Annex	. . .	. . .	. . .
	7	Lough Ree	. . .	. . .	2.50
	8	Cascanuez	. . .	. . .	. . .
	9	Romanium	. . .	. . .	. . .
2/10	1	Beguile	. . .	6.40	4.50
	2	Affius	. . .	. . .	. . .
	4	Cedar Jungle	. . .	7.90	4.80
	5	Melzar	. . .	. . .	. . .
	6	Bold Man	5.50	2.80	2.60
	7	Miss Arlette	$ . . .	$ . . .	$2.50
	8	County Clare	. . .	. . .	. . .
	9	Collision	. . .	. . .	. . .
2/11	1	Fun Lover	. . .	. . .	2.90
	2	Lafourche	. . .	5.10	3.60
	3	Sea Challenge	. . .	. . .	. . .
	4	Shag-Win	. . .	3.70	3.00
	5	Beyond	. . .	2.70	2.30
	6	Oclirock	6.00	3.80	2.60
	7	Resilient	. . .	. . .	. . .
	8	Beau Fond	. . .	. . .	. . .
2/13	1	Assistance	. . .	. . .	. . .
	2	Socko	. . .	3.30	2.70
	3	Snare	. . .	. . .	. . .
	4	White Sails	. . .	. . .	. . .
	5	Fabulous Fox	. . .	. . .	. . .

DATE	RACE	HORSE	WIN	PLACE	SHOW
	6	Whittledy Cut	3.10	2.40	2.40
	7	Shimke	. . .	2.40	2.20
	8	Apollo	. . .	. . .	. . .
	9	Senga	. . .	. . .	4.80
2/14	3	Youngster	. . .	. . .	3.20
	4	Some Crown	. . .	. . .	. . .
	6	Flying Bird	6.30	3.30	2.70
	7	Roman Battle	6.00	3.30	2.90
	8	Intimate	$ 9.30	$ 5.00	$3.80
	9	Overland	. . .	. . .	. . .
2/15	1	Gay Ribbons	. . .	. . .	. . .
	2	The Goon	. . .	. . .	. . .
	4	Haviland	. . .	. . .	. . .
	5	Myrtle	. . .	. . .	. . .
	6	Go Between	. . .	. . .	. . .
	7	Summer Solstice	7.20	3.80	2.70
	8	Fabius	. . .	3.70	2.20
	9	Optimum	. . .	. . .	. . .
2/16	1	Bull-Bys	5.90	3.90	3.00
	2	C. O. Dorsett	. . .	. . .	3.30
	4	Revetment	. . .	. . .	7.90
	6	Nantullah	4.40	2.60	2.40
	7	Rare Treat	. . .	. . .	. . .
	9	Cascanuez	23.90	8.30	7.20
2/17	1	Antique Lady	. . .	. . .	. . .
	2	Namama	. . .	. . .	3.30
	3	East Meadow	4.80	2.70	2.50
	4	Malabar	. . .	. . .	2.80
	5	Jet's War Date	. . .	. . .	. . .
	6	Squared Away	. . .	13.10	7.10
	7	Admiral Vee	. . .	. . .	. . .
	8	Our Dance	. . .	. . .	3.60
	9	Vasco da Gama	. . .	3.30	3.00
2/18	1	Triplerate	$ . . .	$ 6.00	$4.60
	2	Sharpsburg	3.90	2.90	2.40
	3	Nivrag	. . .	4.70	3.30
	4	Doc Walker	. . .	. . .	. . .
	5	Happy New Year	. . .	. . .	. . .
	6	Blacktype	. . .	. . .	. . .

DATE	RACE	HORSE	WIN	PLACE	SHOW
	7	Masked Game	. . .	. . .	. . .
	8	Nashua	2.80	2.30	2.10
2/20	1	Set The Table	14.30	8.30	6.10
	2	Socko	. . .	. . .	2.60
	3	Bingo	. . .	. . .	3.60
	4	Olympia Gal	. . .	4.40	3.80
	5	Dining Alone	. . .	. . .	. . .
	6	Hoop Band	. . .	. . .	. . .
	7	Espea	4.40	3.70	2.80
	8	Blanchard	. . .	. . .	. . .
	9	Buck 'n' Gee	. . .	. . .	. . .
2/21	2	Fun Lover	. . .	. . .	. . .
	4	P.O.Annex	. . .	. . .	. . .
	5	Bugle Call	. . .	3.80	3.20
	6	Fat Boy	. . .	. . .	. . .
	7	Miss Arlette(e) *	3.00	2.70	2.30
	8	Alloyed	. . .	. . .	3.10
	9	Altruistic	5.80	4.40	3.10
2/22	1	Royal Gold	$ . . .	$ . . .	$ . . .
	2	Sea Siren	7.20	4.00	3.20
	3	Busy Harvest	6.50	4.00	3.20
	4	Sweet Sally	. . .	3.50	2.70
	5	Tulchan	. . .	. . .	. . .
	6	The Hon	6.80	3.70	2.20
	7	High Voltage	. . .	5.10	3.80
	8	Beautician	. . .	. . .	2.70
	9	Betsy T.	. . .	8.90	6.40
2/23	1	Johnson T.	. . .	. . .	. . .
	2	Jingler	. . .	. . .	6.50
	3	Miss Blackbird	. . .	. . .	. . .
	5	Mr. Hawley	3.70	2.90	2.60
	6	Cascanuez	. . .	. . .	. . .
	7	Squared Away	10.00	4.60	3.70
	8	G-Two	5.10	3.60	2.90
	9	Beau Diable	5.50	3.80	3.40
2/24	1	Fine Alibi	7.00	4.70	3.50
	2	Bunnie Pete	. . .	5.00	3.50
	3	Olympia Jet	. . .	3.20	2.80
	4	Page One	15.70	8.80	5.80

DATE	RACE	HORSE	WIN	PLACE	SHOW
	5	Snare	13.70	6.30	4.70
	6	Fabulous Fox	4.30	3.20	2.50
	7	Careless Miss	. . .	. . .	2.80
	8	Rockport	$20.50	$ 7.50	$ 4.50
	9	Bootlet	. . .	. . .	. . .
2/25	1	Neversink	. . .	. . .	3.40
	2	Bomb Boo	. . .	. . .	2.40
	3	Do Report	3.10	2.60	2.20
	4	Pintor Lea	3.40	2.50	2.40
	5	Betsy T.	5.50	2.80	2.50
	7	Connie's Pal	18.00	10.70	7.50
	8	Needles	7.20	4.10	3.00
	9	Ludlow	. . .	. . .	. . .
2/27	1	Lafourche	. . .	3.80	2.90
	3	Steps Babe	. . .	. . .	. . .
	4	Glamour	2.80	2.30	2.20
	5	Exclusive	. . .	4.40	3.10
	6	Sweet Sally	3.40	2.50	2.30
	7	Getthere Jack	. . .	2.90	2.50
	8	Ace Captain	. . .	. . .	. . .
	9	Kope's Hope	. . .	. . .	. . .
2/28	1	Antique Lady	. . .	4.00	2.80
	2	Intimate	. . .	. . .	. . .
	5	Bold Hunter	. . .	. . .	. . .
	6	Flying Chief	. . .	. . .	. . .
	7	Lucky Fifteen	. . .	. . .	2.10
	8	Topside	. . .	3.90	3.30
	9	Go Between	. . .	. . .	. . .
2/29	1	Altruistic	$ . . .	$ . . .	$ . . .
	2	Recline	. . .	. . .	. . .
	3	Commodore Curt	. . .	. . .	. . .
	4	A-Pacopep	11.30	5.40	3.60
	5	Jet Action	3.60	2.60	2.20
	6	Alsay	. . .	2.80	2.50
	7	Summer Solstice	. . .	. . .	. . .
	8	Rockport	. . .	4.60	3.30
	9	Yoeman	. . .	. . .	. . .

* Stablemate accounted for placing.

202 plays: 57 won (28%); 92 won or placed, (45.5%); 121 in-the-money, (60%).

Yield: Win, 5%; Place, 2.4%; Show, 3.2%.

Net Profit: Win, $20.50 on $2 flat play; Place, $9.70; Show, $12.90.

The best that can be said for this system is that it's only lukewarm in that it does show a profit in all three categories and therefore would lend itself to pressure betting to force a worthwhile return. Here, we definitely have a small percentage working with us.

However, we don't have to accept anything that's only lukewarm. Certainly it would be foolish to accept it without first reversing chronology.

To do this, we have to make only a few slight changes. For instance, since we will now use earn-ability instead of speed to isolate our contenders, we will need some limits. In the cheaper variety of races, we will consider any horse a contender if he fits in the general group included between the $300 minimum per-race earn-ability and a top limit of $1,000. In the classier races, we will consider only those horses as contenders that have in excess of $1,000 per-race earn-ability.

Of this group of contenders, then, we will take the one having the highest speed rating at today's distance where possible, and on a fast track. If we cannot take a rating at today's distance on a fast track, we will accept a fast track rating on a sprint-for-sprint, and route-for-route basis, making an effort to search out the sprint and/or route closest to today's distance.

When we encounter a class standout, one that has three or more times as much per/race earn-ability than any other horse in the race, we waive the speed factor and insist only that his past performances show some sprint races if this is a sprint and/or route races if this is a route.

Workout Number 2 follows:

WORKOUT #2
(Chronology reversed)

DATE	RACE	HORSE	WIN	PLACE	SHOW
2/1	1	Pass	$ . . .	$ . . .	$ . . .
	2	Whittledy Cut	4.30	3.30	2.60
	4	Most Charming	. . .	13.70	6.10
	5	Squared Away	4.60	3.70	3.00
	6	Tollesboro	. . .	2.50	2.30
	7	Dark Charger	. . .	10.80	8.10
	8	Espea	4.70	3.50	2.70
	9	Topside	7.40	4.10	3.50
2/2	1	Shining Star	. . .	. . .	. . .
	4	Overland	. . .	. . .	. . .
	5	Bold Hunter	. . .	11.00	6.40
	6	Careless Miss	7.80	3.70	3.30
	7	Queen Hopeful	. . .	4.50	3.10
	8	Tournure	. . .	. . .	. . .
	9	Boxer Duke	43.60	19.00	7.80
2/3	2	War Age	4.70	3.30	2.70
	4	Fremarcton	. . .	. . .	. . .
	5	Alsay	. . .	. . .	. . .
	6	Black Record	3.40	2.70	2.20
	7	First Cadet	. . .	. . .	. . .
	8	Dark Ruler	5.80	3.40	2.50
	9	Sea Tale	. . .	7.90	4.50
2/4	1	Regal Favor†	20.70	6.80	3.60
	3	Java Belle	. . .	3.10	2.60
	4	Stevies Pal	. . .	. . .	. . .
	5	Topside	$ . . .	$ 6.40	$ 4.80
	6	Helfast	. . .	. . .	. . .
	7	Lough Ree	13.00	6.20	4.80
	8	Social Outcast	. . .	2.90	2.20
	9	Oclirock	7.20	4.20	3.70
2/6	2	College Chum	. . .	. . .	. . .
	3	Sugarfoot	6.70	4.40	3.20
	4	Cascanuez	3.90	3.40	3.00
	5	Doc Walker	6.00	4.20	2.80
	6	Fabulous Fox	. . .	. . .	2.20
	7	Nail	. . .	. . .	. . .

DATE	RACE	HORSE	WIN	PLACE	SHOW
	8	Kope's Baby(e) *	12.10	10.10	6.00
	9	Calgary	. . .	. . .	. . .
2/7	6	Sometime Thing	3.70	2.30	2.20
	7	Lawless	6.30	4.30	3.20
	8	Go Between	11.50	6.40	5.10
2/8	2	Easy Sweep	30.80	14.60	13.70
	4	Hoop Ring	. . .	2.80	2.50
	5	Hickory Hill	. . .	. . .	3.60
	6	Ifabody	11.80	4.40	3.20
	7	King Hairan	3.20	2.60	2.40
	8	Commodore M.	. . .	3.70	2.50
	9	Gallant Fanar	. . .	. . .	. . .
2/9	1	Caboose	$ . . .	$ . . .	$ 4.10
	2	Dark Patrol	. . .	. . .	. . .
	4	Teri	. . .	. . .	4.30
	5	Key Biscayne	25.00	13.70	7.00
	6	Sagacity	. . .	. . .	. . .
	7	Summer Solstice	4.00	3.70	2.30
	8	Cascanuez	. . .	. . .	. . .
	9	Malabar	. . .	. . .	3.60
2/10	1	Quarter-Master	. . .	. . .	. . .
	4	Tulifiny	. . .	. . .	3.80
	5	Prize Winner	. . .	4.60	3.30
	6	Bold Man	5.50	2.80	2.60
	7	Delta	4.90	3.00	2.30
	8	County Clare	. . .	. . .	. . .
2/11	3	Page One	. . .	. . .	. . .
	5	Royal Oak	6.00	3.00	2.50
	6	The Posse	. . .	5.60	2.80
	7	Resilient	. . .	. . .	. . .
	9	Mr. Jones	11.60	6.20	3.70
2/13	1	Assistance	. . .	. . .	. . .
	3	Snare	. . .	. . .	. . .
	6	Whittledy Cut	3.10	2.40	2.40
	7	Remand	7.20	2.60	2.40
	8	Apollo	. . .	. . .	. . .
	9	For Free	13.60	7.20	4.10
2/14	4	Some Crown	$ . . .	$ . . .	$ . . .

DATE	RACE	HORSE	WIN	PLACE	SHOW
	5	Rockport	8.10	4.40	3.20
	6	Flying Bird	6.30	3.30	2.70
	7	Roman Battle	6.00	3.30	2.90
	8	Intimate	9.30	5.00	3.80
2/15	4	Blue Pharis	. . .	. . .	4.80
	5	Myrtle	. . .	. . .	. . .
	6	Go Between	. . .	. . .	. . .
	7	Trentonian	. . .	. . .	. . .
	8	Call Me Lucky	. . .	. . .	2.10
2/16	1	Bull-Bys**	5.90	3.90	3.00
	2	C. O. Dorsett	. . .	. . .	3.30
	4	Most Charming	. . .	11.20	6.90
	5	Myla	. . .	4.90	4.10
	6	Nantallah	4.40	2.60	2.40
	7	Sometime Thing	3.30	2.60	2.20
	9	Cascanuez	23.90	8.30	7.20
2/17	1	Antique Lady	. . .	. . .	. . .
	3	East Meadow	4.80	2.70	2.50
	4	Ergo	. . .	3.60	2.70
	6	Dark Ruler	. . .	. . .	3.00
	7	Craigwood	7.20	3.20	2.60
	8	Our Dance	. . .	. . .	3.60
	9	Vasco Da Gama	. . .	3.30	3.00
2/18	1	Yoeman	$ 7.30	$ 3.90	$ 3.40
	2	Sharpsburg	3.90	2.90	2.40
	3	Nivrag	. . .	4.70	3.30
	5	Kingmaker	. . .	. . .	2.80
	7	Centennaire	. . .	. . .	. . .
	8	Nashua	2.80	2.30	2.20
	9	Resigned	. . .	. . .	. . .
2/20	1	Set The Table	14.30	8.30	6.10
	3	Final Role	. . .	3.30	2.70
	4	Bull-Bys	. . .	. . .	. . .
	6	Hoop Band	. . .	. . .	. . .
	7	Espea	4.80	3.70	2.80
	8	Blanchard	. . .	. . .	. . .
	9	Buck 'n' Gee	. . .	. . .	. . .
2/21	1	Doctor Dick	. . .	. . .	. . .

DATE	RACE	HORSE	WIN	PLACE	SHOW
	2	War Hawk	4.90	3.30	2.80
	3	Sandersville	. . .	. . .	. . .
	4	Ocean Hop	. . .	. . .	. . .
	5	Mr. Herb A.	9.80	4.30	3.40
	6	Medico	16.00	7.80	4.40
	7	Miss Arlette	3.00	2.70	2.20
	8	Alloyed	. . .	. . .	3.10
	9	Altruistic	5.80	4.40	3.10
2/22	2	Bill's Carol	$ . . .	$ . . .	$ . . .
	3	Busy Harvest	6.50	4.00	3.20
	5	Monogram	5.40	3.10	2.70
	6	The Hon	6.80	3.70	2.20
	7	Sometime Thing	. . .	. . .	2.90
	8	Royal Lark	4.80	3.20	2.60
	9	War Age	6.70	4.60	3.80
2/23	1	Johnson T.	. . .	. . .	. . .
	2	Jingler	. . .	. . .	6.50
	4	Pash Saied	. . .	. . .	2.80
	5	Mr. Hawley	3.70	2.90	2.60
	6	Cascanuez	. . .	. . .	. . .
	7	Black Record	. . .	4.10	3.20
	9	Beau Diable	5.50	3.80	3.40
2/24	1	Barney's Joy	. . .	. . .	4.90
	2	Vanda	. . .	. . .	. . .
	3	Olympia Jet	. . .	3.20	2.80
	5	Queensware	. . .	. . .	. . .
	6	Fabulous Fox	4.30	3.20	2.40
	7	Fantine Busher	4.50	3.20	2.40
	8	Rockport	20.50	7.50	4.50
	9	Par Boy	. . .	3.80	3.20
2/25	1	Set The Table	4.70	3.10	2.50
	3	Do Report	3.10	2.60	2.20
	4	Pintor Lea	$ 3.40	$ 2.50	$ 2.40
	5	Betsy T.	5.50	2.80	2.50
	6	Centennaire	. . .	. . .	. . .
	7	Connie's Pal	18.00	10.70	7.50
	8	Needles	7.20	4.10	3.00
	9	Ludlow	. . .	. . .	. . .

DATE	RACE	HORSE	WIN	PLACE	SHOW
2/27	1	Lafourche	. . .	3.60	2.90
	3	Supreme Music	. . .	. . .	. . .
	4	Glamour	2.80	2.30	2.20
	5	White Orchid	. . .	. . .	. . .
	6	Sweet Sally	3.40	2.50	2.30
	7	Decathlon	6.60	3.00	2.50
2/28	1	Antique Lady	. . .	4.00	2.60
	2	Intimate	. . .	. . .	. . .
	5	Olympia Gal	6.80	3.80	3.30
	7	Lucky Fifteen	. . .	. . .	. . .
	8	Topside	. . .	3.90	3.30
	9	Sam Brook	7.10	3.80	3.10
2/29	1	Ankara	8.10	3.80	3.40
	2	Triplerate	25.70	11.30	6.90
	3	Tiger Dip	. . .	2.90	2.40
	4	A-Pacopep††	11.30	5.40	3.60
	5	Jet Action	3.60	2.60	2.20
	6	Point Of Order	$ 6.00	$ 2.90	$ 2.60
	7	Blue Choir	. . .	. . .	4.00
	8	Roman Princess	. . .	. . .	. . .
	9	Marston Moor	. . .	. . .	. . .

* Took 1¼ M. rating as being closest to today's distance of 1½ M.
** 88 speed rating at today's distance of 7F. Took this as more significant than 88 for Hoop Ring earned at 6F.
† Stablemate accounted for placing.
†† Only one qualified on earn-ability. Excelled on speed.

By reversing our factors, we had 171 plays, 77 of which won (45%); 102 won or placed, (60%); 121 in-the-money, (71%). Net profit on $2 flat play to win, $305.90; place, $148.50; show, $82.50. Yield: Win, 86.5%; Place, 39.8%; Show, 24.1%. By chronology, then, a lukewarm system becomes a powerhouse.

15. Graded Race System

Let's see if we can make a bob off the beetles by being unconventional. Straying from the straight and narrow path of straight handicapping can sometimes be fun, and if there's an honest buck to be had, well, why not?

The main virtue of this system, aside from its simplicity and ease of operation, is that it has a tendency dear to the longshot player's heart. The prices it snags on occasion would make even a chalk player say "Wow!" Incidentally, if there are any confirmed chalk players among us, and there's always at least one in every party, better let some of this plan rub off on you. There's nothing a chalk player needs more than an occasional price, and though he can point to a higher win percentage than we can hope for with this one, it will do something playing chalk can never accomplish and this is show a profit.

Class and condition, both evaluated in a loose, disjointed sort of way, will be the meat of this system, though neither will be delineated in the exacting manner employed in our handicap-analysis. Nor will our class efforts be as fruitless as trying to outguess trainer manipulations in the claimers, or trying to evaluate the differences between allowance races, or grading handicaps and stakes. Instead we are going to rough-grade the races in such a manner as to get a sort of "class by association." This will be accomplished by simple addition and the sum shall never exceed 21.

For instance, it will be conceded, no doubt, that the lowest level of competition on any afternoon's card, is usually found in the daily double duo, the first and second races. The calibre of competition improves from here up to and including the feature race which is the sixth at some tracks but most usually the seventh. This is the cream of the competition for the afternoon whether it be the Derby or a claimer with fancy tags. Then the quality of the competition regresses again, so that we will regard race number eight as about the equal of number four, and race number nine about equal to three. This is the general rule by which we'll work, though you'll be able to find exceptions to it if you look hard enough.

Now then, to get the class, or grade, of a contestant, we are going to be interested in the race numbers in which he ran in his last three starts. These are the small superior figures immediately following the date of the race and immediately preceding the track abbreviation.

To get the grade of this particular contestant, we simply add together these most recent three race numbers regardless of distance or track condition. We use the numerals as we find them up to and including the seventh race. For the eighth race we allow 4, and for the ninth race, 3. At no time, then, can any horse receive a sum greater than 21, and this only if all of his last three races were run as the seventh race.

To demonstrate the logic behind this, let's exaggerate an example. Let's say we have a hide that has been appearing regularly in the seventh race, the feature. Today he is shifted to one of the Daily Double pair. Even if he had not been making out well as a feature racer, his class by association is definitely better than that of the normal Daily Double racer.

In our race to race application, a nag with a grade of 21

can be considered of higher quality than a horse with a grade of 10, or 15, etc. So in selecting our contenders we will accept all those horses with a point grade falling within a three point spread of the highest grade for the race. For instance, if the highest grade proves to be 17, then all horses having grades between 14 and 17 will be contenders, which we will separate on a present condition basis.

This, we have also simplified for use in system play: In the *Form*, between the weight column and the jockey column, there are four "calls" giving the running position of the horse at that point in the race. We are interested only in the first two of these "calls." A contender must have been running either first, second or third at *both* of these first two calls for us to rate him as sharp, or approaching the kind of sharpness of value to us. In case more than one contender qualifies under these rules, we will make a further separation by taking the one which finished closest to the winner in his last (most recent) race. We will not accept for play a horse that won his last start.

The initial step, selecting contenders by grade numbers, takes only a couple of minutes for each race. The separation of contenders is accomplished by only a glance at the first two call positions, and then at the finish position to make sure he didn't win that last race. To emphasize, the isolation of contenders requires the use of the most recent three races. The separation of contenders on our condition basis will utilize only the last start.

Occasionally, we will find a race in which there is only one contender, all the rest of the contestants having grade numbers below the three-point spread. In such a case, we accept the lone contender for play with or without the condition factor, requiring only that he must have started at this track during the current meeting. *Any* contender must meet this require-ment in order to become a qualified play.

Let's look at a couple of races included in the workout. In the first race at Sunshine Park, February 1, 1956, we have five contenders after adding race numbers together. Thirteen (13) was the highest grade number, so we included all horses graded between 13 and 10.

Prize Ticket (3-5-5)	13
Blue Quail (9-9-7)	13
Platterette (5-2-5)	12
Time For Fun (2-5-9)	10
Wild Risk (3-8-3)	10

The disqualified horses at this point were Wing Kitty (8); Hurbane (8); Lady Flushing (7); Merry Chant (6); and Halbel (5).

Of those qualified according to grade, Prize Ticket has been out at the current meeting, but was running seventh at both of the first two calls in his last race. We toss him out. Blue Quail, also out at the meeting but was running fourth at the first call though she did move into third place by the time she got to the pre-stretch (second) call. We can't use her, either. Platterette had been out at the meeting, but was unable to do better than sixth at both of the first two calls in that last race. Time For Fun had not been out since August (six months) at Haggerstown. He goes into the discard. Wild Risk was on the pace (leading) in the first call here at the current meeting. She was holding second at pre-stretch call. We see that we have a qualified play after checking and finding she did not win her last start.

Platterette and Halbel got the heavy play. The two-buck improvers of the breed were so busy chunking it in on these two they completely overlooked Wild Risk. So she took the waltz wire to wire. Her mutuel was $152.30, 38.30, and $12.80 across the board. Platterette challenged in the stretch but Wild Risk wasn't to be refused.

In the second race, after grading, we found ourselves with

six contenders, the high grade again being 13 points. The six were: Raggylug (13); Blue Teal (13); Bob O Boy (12); Hello Pudgy (12); Badger (11); and Brownskin (10).

Three of these, Bob O Boy, Brownskin, and Badger, had been running first, second or third in each of their respective last races. The rest were eliminated on this point. Of the three still qualifying, Badger was unraced since November at Churchill Downs. We discard him and now we have only Brownskin and Bob O Boy to separate by the tied contender rule. Brownskin was beaten seven and three-quarters lengths by the winner of his last race. Bob O Boy was subdued by six in his last. Bob O Boy gets the nod as the remaining qualifier. Another winner.

Now let's look at the sixth race on the same day. After grading, we have only two contenders: Just Barbara (20); and Herb S. (19). Both have been out at the current SP meeting, and both qualify on the rule requiring them to be running forwardly at the first two calls. Herb S. won his last race. Just Barbara did not, so she was the qualified play. She won.

One more example. We're still at SP on Feb. 1. There are eight starters in the eighth race. A Gem has sixteen grade points, while the next closest are Dom W. and Lautenberg, with eleven points each. Since it would take a five-point spread to include these as contenders, instead of the three-point spread we allow, we have A Gem standing all alone on grade. We do not need to qualify him on condition. Since he's so obviously spotted just right for a win, it would seem unrealistic not to trust the trainer to have his horse in shape. Why should he waste a spot like this on an unfit horse?

At the end of this chapter, we'll make a separate workout of these outstanding spots (like A Gem) for comparison, and for the busy businessman who "likes to have something going" once in a while.

Here's what happened:

WORKOUT #1

DATE	RACE	HORSE	WIN	PLACE	SHOW
2/1	1	Wild Risk	$152.30	$38.30	$12.80
	2	Bob O Boy	7.90	4.00	2.60
	4	Jimmy's First	4.60	2.80	2.60
	6	Just Barbara	8.20	3.80	3.00
	7	Sunday Favor	. . .	. . .	. . .
	8	A Gem	18.40	4.40	3.40
2/2	1	Speedy Van	$ . . .	$ 9.50	$ 4.90
	3	Nile Prince	. . .	. . .	. . .
	4	Treadmill	8.20	5.00	3.20
	5	Coruscate	. . .	. . .	. . .
	6	Rags	. . .	2.90	2.20
	7	Beeston	10.10	4.90	4.10
	8	Taunting Beau	. . .	. . .	2.10
	9	Party King	. . .	6.30	2.90
2/3	1	Li'l Mick	. . .	. . .	. . .
	2	Saucy Me	. . .	. . .	. . .
	5	Mackey Bot	26.30	6.70	4.00
	6	Red Petticoat	. . .	. . .	. . .
	7	Destino Miss	. . .	. . .	. . .
	9	Secret Impulse	. . .	. . .	. . .
2/4	2	Heureux	. . .	. . .	. . .
	3	Treadmill*	. . .	. . .	. . .
	6	Daring Spirit	11.30	4.60	2.60
	7	Bright Penny	. . .	. . .	. . .
	8	Lucious Fruit	. . .	. . .	. . .
	9	Soakin' Wet	. . .	. . .	. . .
2/6	2	Myrna Arlene	. . .	. . .	. . .
	5	Straight Wire	. . .	. . .	. . .
	6	Wynn's Due	. . .	. . .	. . .
	9	Moon Of Hearts	. . .	3.90	2.60
2/7	1	Dark Pride	$ . . .	$ . . .	$ . . .
	2	Golden Blossom	. . .	. . .	. . .
	3	Grey Granite	12.40	4.50	3.50
	4	Blue Whiz Kid	. . .	. . .	. . .
	5	Solero Jr.	. . .	5.20	4.00

DATE	RACE	HORSE	WIN	PLACE	SHOW
	6	Romp And Play	. . .	. . .	3.80
	7	Red Petticoat	. . .	. . .	. . .
	9	Polar Region	14.70	7.30	3.50
2/8	1	Nell Keegan	. . .	. . .	. . .
	3	Miss Allright	. . .	. . .	. . .
	5	Runebb's Lad	. . .	. . .	. . .
	6	Herb S.	4.70	3.40	2.70
	7	Brassy Miss	. . .	3.50	2.50
	8	Cross End	. . .	. . .	. . .
	9	Cable Flag	. . .	. . .	. . .
2/9	3	McGinnis	5.30	5.00	2.80
	5	Arthur Itis	. . .	. . .	. . .
	7	Tetrabasic	12.10	5.80	3.00
2/10	1	Mr. Puddy Cat	5.70	3.20	2.90
	2	Thisbe	. . .	. . .	6.30
	5	Betty's Lass	. . .	. . .	. . .
	8	Sam Park	. . .	. . .	. . .
2/11	2	Jolie B.	. . .	. . .	. . .
	3	Solero Jr.	. . .	. . .	2.90
	5	Destino Miss	4.90	3.20	2.80
	6	Indian Lad	$ . . .	$ 3.40	$ 2.50
2/13	1	Cross End	8.70	5.10	3.70
	5	Royal Charles	10.30	5.00	2.90
	6	Dom W.	. . .	. . .	. . .
	7	Not Bad	. . .	. . .	. . .
	8	Extra Five	. . .	. . .	. . .
	9	Fithian	. . .	9.70	6.10
2/14	1	Sky Shoot	. . .	. . .	11.20
	3	Taxas Ike	. . .	. . .	. . .
	5	Rival Time	. . .	. . .	. . .
	8	Batavia Belle	. . .	. . .	. . .
	9	Party King	5.60	3.10	3.00
2/15	1	Clouded Sun	9.70	3.70	3.80
	3	Burnt Muffet	. . .	. . .	. . .
	4	Doctor Ray	16.90	7.60	9.10
	5	Extra Five	. . .	. . .	. . .
	7	Rock Dozer	. . .	. . .	. . .

DATE	RACE	HORSE	WIN	PLACE	SHOW
	8	Sent Back	. . .	. . .	. . .
	9	Uncle Edgar	. . .	. . .	. . .
2/16	3	Wynn's Due	. . .	. . .	. . .
	4	Baker's Hornet	. . .	. . .	. . .
	5	Boss Bennie	5.50	3.60	2.50
	7	Flying Record	. . .	. . .	2.60
	9	Attention Mark	. . .	3.00	2.50
2/17	1	Changeaway	$ . . .	$ . . .	$ . . .
	2	Kate's Rebel	5.20	3.50	2.70
	4	Propeller	9.00	3.90	3.20
	5	Enterpriser	. . .	. . .	. . .
	6	Beeston	. . .	. . .	. . .
	8	Calico Creek	13.30	5.80	4.70
2/18	2	Mahatma II	. . .	. . .	. . .
	3	Flaneur	. . .	. . .	. . .
	4	Green Cross	4.90	3.80	3.50
	5	Pat's Valentine	5.50	3.50	2.80
	6	Romp And Play	. . .	. . .	5.20
	7	D'Arbonne	. . .	6.20	6.20
	9	Polar Region	. . .	11.00	6.40
2/20	1	Stewy	. . .	. . .	. . .
	2	Kamloops	. . .	. . .	. . .
	4	Casey's Error	5.70	3.00	2.30
	6	Pennfleur	. . .	3.80	2.70
	7	Golden Whirl	. . .	5.50	2.50
2/21	1	Coruscate	6.60	3.70	3.40
	2	Challcote	. . .	. . .	. . .
	4	Shooting Box	. . .	4.20	3.30
	5	Eugene Boy	5.10	3.30	2.90
	7	Top Again	5.20	3.50	2.70
	8	Roz's Pride	. . .	. . .	. . .
	9	Rocket Blue	. . .	. . .	. . .
2/22	1	Big Trick	$ . . .	$ . . .	$ . . .
	2	Depal	. . .	. . .	. . .
	4	Mackey Boy	. . .	. . .	2.80
	5	Dancing Marjie	8.00	4.70	3.20
	7	Haydon	. . .	. . .	. . .
	9	Army Pal	. . .	. . .	. . .

DATE	RACE	HORSE	WIN	PLACE	SHOW
2/23	1	Jubilee	. . .	2.70	2.40
	2	De Music	. . .	. . .	. . .
	3	Len-a-Chance	7.50	4.60	4.10
	4	Battle Cjief	8.10	3.70	2.40
	6	Light Don	. . .	. . .	7.50
	8	Silent Mirth	. . .	. . .	. . .
	9	Polar Region	. . .	. . .	. . .
2/24	1	Mr. Dude	. . .	. . .	. . .
	3	Gray Vision	. . .	. . .	. . .
	4	Runebb's Son	. . .	. . .	. . .
	5	Count Pur	7.90	4.10	3.00
	6	Get Busy	. . .	3.00	2.60
	7	Bewitching	. . .	. . .	. . .
	8	Joyce Gober	. . .	2.80	2.80
	9	Slide Rock	. . .	. . .	. . .
2/25	1	Hawthorn	. . .	2.70	2.50
	3	Jimmy's First	. . .	. . .	. . .
	4	Reveille	5.40	3.70	2.80
	5	Golden Whirl	$ . . .	$ . . .	$ . . .
	6	Nero's Mermaid	. . .	. . .	6.20
	7	Rock Pilot	4.50	3.90	2.70
	8	Mr. T. A.	. . .	. . .	. . .
	9	Gerry Grayson	. . .	. . .	. . .
2/27	1	Cap Checker	. . .	. . .	. . .
	3	Sun Crisp	. . .	. . .	. . .
	4	Foxie Flag	29.10	11.40	6.30
	5	Pennfleur	. . .	3.40	2.60
	8	Andromeda	14.80	7.30	3.90
	9	Bob F.	. . .	. . .	. . .
2/28	1	Cold Water	4.60	3.70	2.50
	2	High View Don	. . .	. . .	. . .
	3	Jubilee	. . .	. . .	2.30
	5	Royal Charles	. . .	. . .	. . .
	6	Mab	. . .	. . .	. . .
	8	Tetrabasic	. . .	. . .	. . .
	9	Piparoo	5.60	3.80	2.80
2/29	3	Halara	. . .	. . .	. . .
	4	Sergeant Spook	. . .	6.20	3.00

DATE	RACE	HORSE	WIN	PLACE	SHOW
	5	Lasting Spring	. . .	. . .	. . .
	6	Nero's Mermaid	. . .	. . .	. . .
	8	Party King	. . .	. . .	. . .
	9	Fred B.	6.60	4.40	3.00

* Treadmill, in the third race on February 4, was returning to the races as a previous winner. Though I knew he won his last race (see fourth race on February 2 of the workout) the Miami edition of the *Form* showed him as having run second, so I included him even though he should not have been qualified for play.

In breaking the workout down, we find that we had 152 plays during the month. That's plenty of action for anyone. Forty-two of them won (28%). But then, with such a loose, easy system, we hardly expected a high percentage of winners. However, we did expect some good prices, and we got them. So our net profit on two-buck flat bets to win was $222.40. There was also a small profit from place play, $11.40, while the show gave a loss of $32.40.

So this is strictly a win system, and our yield in this category was a big, fat 73% on total invested capital.

Now let's take a look at the results obtained from our spot-play system, those grade number standouts which excelled over the rest of their respective fields by more than a three-point spread. We made no attempt to qualify these beasties on the condition factor, remember.

WORKOUT #2
(Grade Standouts)

DATE	RACE	HORSE	WIN	PLACE	SHOW
2/1	9	A Gem	$18.40	$ 4.40	$3.40
2/2	3	Nile Prince	. . .	. . .	. . .
2/6	2	Myrna Arlene	. . .	. . .	. . .
2/7	4	Blue Whiz Kid	. . .	. . .	. . .
	5	Solero Jr.	. . .	5.20	4.00
2/10	8	Sam Park	. . .	. . .	. . .
2/11	2	Jolie B.	. . .	. . .	. . .

DATE	RACE	HORSE	WIN	PLACE	SHOW
2/13	9	Fithian	. . .	9.70	6.10
2/16	5	Boss Bennie	5.50	3.60	2.50
2/17	4	Propeller	9.00	3.90	3.20
2/20	2	Kamloops	. . .	. . .	. . .
2/21	2	Challcote	. . .	. . .	. . .
2/22	2	Depal	. . .	. . .	. . .
2/23	3	Len-a-Chance	7.50	4.60	4.40
2/27	4	Foxie Flag	29.10	11.40	6.30
2/28	5	Royal Charles	. . .	. . .	. . .
2/29	9	Fred B.	6.60	4.40	3.00

Our spots, being more selective, gave us 17 plays for the month. Six of these won (35%), which is a step-up in win percentage over the number one system of some 7%. And the yield moved up from 73% to 124%.

So between the two systems, there's profit for both the action fans and the spot players.

16. Taming the Double

Since approximately 60% of the 39 million hoss fans go for the Daily Double, that fabulous bargain basement gimmick conceived by some money-happy genius some years back to bolster the slim mutuel play in the early stanzas of most any man's track, mine would be the still small voice in the wilderness if I attempted to argue against it. Instead, after considerable soul-searching and brain-picking, I decided to see what could be done about taking the thing off the sucker list and adding it to the good speculation side of the ledger.

The Daily Double, for you newcomers, is a form of two-horse parlay in which the player, for the bargain price of two bucks, can attempt to pick the winners in both the first and second races—no mean feat considering the doubtful calibre of the competition. More often than not, these races are filled from the chaff of Shed Row. But even the beetles have to be given a chance at a purse, and there's got to be a winner in every race. All we have to do is figure a way to nail them down.

Our biggest asset is price, for one seldom sees a really slim Doubles payoff. The average is very good and four figure payoffs are relatively commonplace, with the record being twelve thousand-odd bucks for two established a few years back at Tijuana.

However, we don't need anything like four figure payoffs to make a sound speculation of the Daily Double. All we need is a couple of average-sized payoffs per week and we've got it made.

The Daily Double fields usually fill to capacity with, more often than not, a few extras shuffled in by way of a mutuel field. This makes for crowding, bumping, and various and assorted traffic problems. This, combined with the fact we want price, dictates an elastic selection medium and multiple coverage.

There is only one way to be sure of winning the Double every day in the week, and that's by buying the board. But if it were as easy as that everybody with a few hundred bucks operating capital would be beating the Double and living high off the hog. However, we've learned enough about picking them by now so that we could snag three likely contenders in the first race to wheel with a like number in the second stanza without requiring Fort Knox to finance our play, and with a reasonable expectation of finding ourselves with the right combination in our hot little hand at least a couple of times a week. We'd even settle for one of those fat ones a week.

So let's see how we make out with a not-too-exhausting search on the basis of the two main factors as discussed in our chapter on handicap-analysis. Since we want to woo price, we might defeat our purpose if we demand too much in qualifying our plays. So, let's set our procedure up in this way:

1) Wherever possible, our three contenders will be those having the best per-race earn-ability.

2) Where this is impracticable, as in the case of maidens, mostly the two-year-olds just getting started in their racing careers, we will use our speed standards either on recent races, if any, or workouts.

Let's look in on that first week of racing again at Hialeah, since the work we already did there should be fresh in the student-handicapper's mind.

On February 1, 1957, we get left at the post because Mark's Puzzle, winner of the first half of the D.D. Duo, was a few bucks outside the pale on per-race earn-ability, unless taken from his two races in 1957. You will remember we had to resort to this in our original analysis, but we're not resorting to detailed analysis here, so let's just accept our loss in the first and go on to the second day. After all, we only had $18.00 invested as we'd have been required to play Setubal, Terrapin, and Rare Vintage in the first race wheeled with Tender Morsel, Salmative, and Kismiss in the second half. This requires nine combinations at two dollars a throw: Setubal and Tender Morsel; Setubal and Salmative; Setubal and Kismiss—that's three combos. Terrapin and Tender Morsel; Terrapin and Salmative; and Terrapin and Kismiss—that's six combos. Rare Vintage and Tender Morsel; Rare Vintage and Salmative; and Rare Vintage and Kismiss—that's nine combos.

On the second day, the three earn-ability horses in the first race were Elliott's Gem, Don't Look Now, and Big Billie. In the second race, a maiden affair for three-year-olds, among them some first-time starters that will have to be rated from workouts. We are in a much better position in a situation of this kind than the selector who does not have our speed standards.

On speed then, our three contenders in the second race on February 2nd are Moon Crazy, Royal Brick, and Royal Envoy. This time we have the right answer among our nine combinations, for Big Billie copped the first, and Royal Envoy showed them the way home in the second. The most of the cash customers must have been looking the other way for the payoff was good—$174.20, $138.20 of which is profit for two day's operation.

On the third day, February 4, 1957, earn-ability supplies us with our three contenders in the first race. They are Gotta-passem, Mighty Turf, and Milk Baron. These we wheel to Grand Daze, Baker Street, and Son o' Doge in the second half. Once again we have the right combo in our ticket on the Milk Baron-Grand Daze team. This Double pasteboard was worth $416.50 at the cashier's window, and our profit for three days is $536.70. We've already got our coupla winners for the week, but let's run it out and see what happens.

On the fourth day of our racing week, February 5, our three contenders in the first race, on earn-ability, were Blue Guy, Altruistic, and Getthere Frank. The second was one of those horrible four-year-old maiden affairs with too many of them having no earnings whatsoever. So we resort to speed, and even this is rather disheartening. But by resorting to workouts where past performances were too many months old to mean anything, we come up with Fiddlin' Son (−5); Googin (−1); and Ever More (0).

The combo of Blue Guy and Fiddlin' Son came through with a successful joint effort and the reward to the faithful was $62.70, all but $18 of which was profit.

The fifth day of our six day racing week gave us three more earn-ability nags in the first race: Semolina; Diavolezza; and Commaria. These we wheel to another batch of three-year-old maidens in the second. With the use of our speed standards we finally isolate Jedgar Ruler, Trireme and True Verdict. We took the latter over Destined Hour because True Verdict had $200 earn-ability whereas Destined Hour had no earnings.

The team of Commaria-Jedgar Ruler was worth $55.50 at the D.D. cashier's window.

We get Chanter, Go Between, and Tombouctu as our three earn-ability hides in the first race of the sixth day of our racing week. These we wheel to a band of three-year-old maiden fillies. (You get to playing the Double and you draw the line at nothing.) Rating the works, we get Discriminate, Neshanic, and Double Danger.

We misfired in the first race here, as Double Bogey copped this one and left our combo high and dry, but we had a net of $600.90 for the week, and four successful combo's out of six tries.

To give the thin view of the picture, the same period produced a profit of only $36.10 at Sunshine Park. We had two winners out of six tries here, which would have been all right except that one of them was only $14.00, the other $130.10.

Nevertheless, your average should hold up very well over a reasonable period of time. The lean weeks will be rounded out by the fat ones.

17. Grading the Tracks

Some pessimist once stated there are a thousand ways to lose a horse race. I wonder if his estimate included just plain old wrong selections—the kind any fan is apt to make until he becomes aware of the fact that not all mile ovals, or all so-called major tracks, necessarily cater to the same quality of racer.

We have already seen how erroneous speed ratings can be when figured from track records for the simple but obvious reason that the records at the cheap tracks are made by cheap horses—horses that are running cheap because they are slow—and therefore any records they set are inferior when observed alongside those set by the champs and near-champs. Many a hoss race has been lost by the fan who believed that a 99 was a helluva speed rating without regard to where it was made.

Another fallacy which has put many a fan on a wrong horse, is the assumption that a $2500 claimer, for instance, is the same no matter where it's run. Or that an allowance racer from the leaky-roof circuit is the same as an allowance racer at Santa Anita. Or that handicaps and stakes are just that, no matter where carded.

It is true these are listed merely as such-and-such-amount claimers in the *Form* without any warning that all that is labeled the same is not necessarily anything but a very distant cousin. The *Form* doesn't say in so many words that the allowance (Alw) race run at the half-mile bull ring is not the equivalent to that one you're comparing it with, which was run at Belmont. They're both labeled "(Alw)," aren't they? And that stakes champ from Pomona . . . how come he can't even get a piece of the purse of the lowest-priced claimer at Hollywood Park—if he could even get stable space there in the first place?

To a gratifying degree we have taken the curse off this problem by the use of per-race earn-ability, even as we rejected the false speed ratings for those figured from standards. However, the fan cannot know too much about the mediums through which he expects to speculate. He should be able to tell almost at a glance at the class line whether this horse is slumming, consorting with his own kind, or is a visiting fireman in over his head.

To assist in this identification, I am offering a partial list of tracks graded according to purse distribution, for it stands to reason that the better horses are going to be shipped where the better purses prevail. If a horse is capable of winning $4,500 purses, his owner is not going to risk sending him out after nine-hundred-dollar purses.

This is especially true of the so-called summer tracks, where an owner or trainer has his choice of literally dozens of different grade tracks in operation at one time. It is less true of the winter tracks, where the horsemen do not have this wide choice. This latter point, however, has a tendency to make selecting, for the average fan, even more difficult at the winter tracks. The horses more or less gravitate to their true levels in the summer months. At the winter ovals, a smattering of all kinds are mixed together, and until they have been out against each other often enough to allow for a horse-to-horse analysis, it's apt to be pretty tough pickin's for those struggling speculators who don't know as much as you and I about how to handle the problem.

Our Grade #1 tracks, and these gradings were made from the run-of-the-mill purses, exclusive of the stakes offerings, because it is from these more or less ordinary races that the vast majority of our action comes: Aqu.; Bel.; SA; Jam.; Mth.

Grade #2: Hia.; Hol.; Sar.; Del.; Atl.; G.S.

Grade #3: Trp.; G.P.; Was.; Haw.; Pim.; Bow.; Lrl.

Grade #4: Nar.

Grade #5: Kee.; Det.; Suf.; C.D.; L.D.; Spt.; Rkm.; G.G.; B.M.; Dmr.

Grade #6: Ran.; H.P.

Grade #7: F.G.; Tdn.

Grade #8: F.P.

Grade #9: R.D.

Grade #10: S.P.; C.T.; Beu.; Whe.; Crn.

This list is not complete, but it should give you a pretty fair cross section from which to grade the tracks in your locality. The above, you might say, are the key tracks, though any of them are subject to change as run-of-the-mill purses change.

What value has all this? How can we use it? To make a hypothetical case. Supposing we're at Sunshine Park, a Grade #10 track, and in looking over the past performances we see a horse entered and recently raced at Hialeah, a Grade #2 track. Has this horse been racing over his head at Hialeah, or has his owner simply vanned him the two-hundred-odd miles across the state for a melon cutting?

He may have looked bad in his recent races at Hialeah in that elite company, but his speed and earn-ability figures may be comparable with those of the other SP entries. The drop in grade of competition could well make him a double-locked cinch. On the other hand, if his figures are not comparable, better let him run once in this cheaper company. It could be his owner vanned him over here in desperation.

Or suppose we're at Aqueduct and we have a horse that figures pretty well off his races at Rockingham. This is a Grade #5 horse moving up into Grade #1 company. His claiming tag or other class line might make him appear to be equal to this competition, but until he has proven he can run with this kind, better regard him with suspicion.

On the other hand, maybe his past performances show he raced well at Belmont before being shipped to Rockingham. Maybe the owner shipped him to try to snag a little purse money in the easier races at the Rock while his horse was below peak form. In this instance, we know the horse to be a Grade #1 performer, and now that he's back from his Grade #5 slumming, he deserves serious consideration.

Or track grading can often be used to good advantage where we have a tie between two or more contenders, or they might just figure close enough so that none constitutes a good betting medium on figures. If the past performances of one shows creditable races at a Grade #3 track, let's say, while the other's background record was made at Raton, the Grade #3 racer suddenly emerges as a standout play.

Another way this can prove valuable is to use it in conjunction with the race grading. Let's say we have two contestants, both with good records, but Horse A has been campaigning at Monmouth, a Grade #1 track, while Horse B has been running at Delaware, a Grade #2 track. At first blush, Horse A might seem to be the play—until we discover he has been entered consistently in the early races (1, 2, or 3) while Horse B was a feature racer (6 and/or 7) at the Grade #2 track. There should be no question, in this case, that the Grade #2 racer will take the Grade #1 nag.

There's one more thought I want to leave with the student-analyst. Suppose you are considering two horses that are tied on earn-ability. The first one earned his per-race average at a Grade #1 track, and the second earned his at a Grade #5 track. Could there be any doubt in your mind that the Grade #1 racer had earned his in harder competition than the other and could therefore be awarded the edge in class?

Do you remember Duke's Sandal, whom the two-buck bettors made a false favorite in one of our earlier examples? This was at Hialeah, a Grade #2 track, and almost all the contestants were first or second grade, but Duke's Sandal, the only win (in fact the only in-the-money effort) shown in his past performances was in Grade #7 company at Thistledowns, and in the third race at that. If the fans had been familiar with track grading, and understood its potential, do you think they could have made Duke's Sandal favorite against the eventual winner, On Her Way, who had two good wins at Grade #2 Garden State, and had just run second at first asking at Hialeah, and with a very creditable effort in a HcpS at Monmouth, a Grade #1 track.

It will pay you to know your track grades, and it will help impress them on your mind if you'll work them out for your local circuit yourself.

18. One-Two-Three System

Here is a simple little plan designed for the occasional holiday or Saturday fan. It is another of the variety which demands absolutely no handicapping or figuring on the part of the speculator. By figuring, we mean interpretation of past performances. There is, actually, a little simple arithmetic involved, but only in connection with the betting plan which is the most important part of this little gem.

For our selections, we're going to rely on Sweep in the *Daily Racing Form*. Since he is the price line maker and graded handicapper of the *Racing Form* experts, we'll assume he's considered the best. For that matter we don't have to have the best, just any reasonably good selector who can come up with a winner or two during the afternoon. If he's a longshot picker, one winner will be enough. If not, he ought to be able to come up with a couple.

So, we'll settle on Sweep for our workout to see if this idea has any merit. And we'll take his top selection after scratches, and we'll start right with the first race of the afternoon. Our first bet will be four dollars, two two-buck ducats.

How did we arrive at that? That is where our 1-2-3 system of wagering comes in. You start your play by writing down those three digits: 1-2-3. The first bet, then is the sum of the first and last digits, 1 and 3, or $4.00. If we get a winner, we cross off the two end digits. If we get a loser we add the amount of the lost bet to the right hand end of the line of uncrossed digits and proceed as before to arrive at the amount of our next bet. At any time we show a profit of six units ($6.00 in this case), we are through with this series and start a fresh one. At any time our play reaches approximately $20.00 on the profit side, we are through for the day. This leaves no decision for the fan to make. The size of his bets are regulated for him. Starting and stopping time are prearranged for him. All he has to do is be able to add the two small end numbers, the ones left after the previous play.

So let's presume that Sweep missed the first race. Our series going into the second would read thus: 1-2-3-4, and the bet would be the sum of the end numbers 1 and 4, or $5.00. So let's say we hit the second. We then cross out both end numbers and our series looks like this: 2-3. Thus, if we have not already made our $6.00 profit, we continue the series by adding the two uncrossed end numbers, 2 and 3. And our third bet would be $5.00.

Simple, isn't it? We cross off *two* digits each time we get a winner, but only add *one* digit after a loss. Any time our prices are so small (about even money) that we have to run our series all the way out until all numbers are crossed off, our profit will be $6.00, if all payoffs were exactly even money, or $4.00 on the tote board. We will never risk running a series on up just because there are some unused numbers still left in it when we already have a minimum of $6.00 profit. The old series has served its purpose. We start fresh, and then only if our total profit for the day has not yet reached $20.00. If it has, we fold up and go home and brag to the neighbors about our winnings.

So we're ready to go to work and run off a few days just

to prove it works. Let's start with blue Monday at Gulfstream Park on March 11, 1957.

Sweep's top selection in the first race is Revolark. Our beginning series is 1-2-3. We play $4.00 to win on Revolark.

The 7.10 mutuel gives $14.20 gross return for our two tickets, of which $10.20 is profit. Since this is in excess of $6.00, we are through with this series. Sweep's top selection in the second race is Free And Busy, and our bet, from the new series, is $4.00. But Free And Busy does not choose to run, so we add the lost four dollars to the right hand end of the series. Here's what we have going into the third race: 1-2-3-4 and our $5.00 wager on Trumpington is derived as usual, by adding the first and last numbers together.

Again we have a loser, so the amount of the lost bet goes onto the right hand end of the series: 1-2-3-4-5, and our bet is $6.00 on Chateau, which is Sweep's top selection in the fourth race. According to the chart writer, Chateau lacked a rally. Anyhow, we lacked a win, so the series builds up: 1-2-3-4-5-6.

Thus, we find ourselves with a $7.00 wager on War Command in the fifth. Finical set all the pace to the half where War Command took over and never left the issue in doubt thereafter. He paid $7.80. Our gross for seven bucks worth of pasteboards, was $27.30. *But*—we have $22.00 invested in this series, so our net is $5.30, and our profit for five races, $5.30 plus $10.20 or $15.50.

All right. If you're the conservative type, go on home. But the system rules permit us to keep on until we have approximately twenty dollars, so we cross off the two end numbers of our series (since we didn't quite realize a profit of $6.00). On the other hand, if you think $5.30 is close enough to $6.00 for practical purposes, ditch the old series and start a new one. Be just as flexible as you want to be. The rules, such as they are, need not be absolutely binding, but are set up as guide posts. Anyhow, we'll continue with the old series: 2-3-4-5. Our end numbers are 2 and 5, so our bet is $7.00, and Sweep's top pick in the sixth is Cedrus.

Here again we have a successful speculation when Cedrus wrested command, in the stretch, from Ratheram, under energetic urging by Jockey Joe Culmone. The payoff was $5.40. The gross on our $7.00 investment was $18.90, and the profit $11.90. For the day, we now have a profit of $27.40. Time to depart.

Personally, I have a natural distrust of public selectors, so feel the fan would be much better off making his own selections either by handicap-analysis, or through the use of one of the other systems. Certainly he has a better chance for price as most of the public selectors' pix are apt to be underlaid and we're always concerned with beating the price. However, the 1-2-3 System relies more on the betting plan than on the selection medium, so if you want to avoid work, pick your own selector, either one of the *Form* or *Telegraph* experts or some local newspaper selector you feel can come up with a couple of winners consistently, and let the mutuels fall where they may.

19. Money Control

Any *modus operandi* can be said to be made up of two general parts, the selection medium and the wagering plan. It is important that each is suited to the other, and to the operator and the size of bankroll available.

We have already investigated two different betting plans, both of which are strong. In the Hit and Run System, the size of our wager at all times was controlled by the odds with the goal in view of a daily minimum wage. This, in effect, was a progression-regression proposition according to odds quoted at the moment.

In the 1-2-3 System the amounts of our wagers was controlled at all times by the status of the series of numbers at that time, i.e., the sum of the uncrossed end numbers. This method of money control will work equally well on both win and place wagering, since we can usually expect an average place price of four dollars or better. It would not be so effective for the show because of the high percentage of hits at considerably below the four-dollar mark. However, if you happen to dream up a system that would hold up to four dollars or better for the show, the 1-2-3 control would be very effective.

Now let's consider percentage wagering which can be used to good advantage for win, place or show action. Percentage wagering is at its best where the operator has a limited capital which he is anxious to build up as quickly and safely as possible. Once, as an experiment, I ran a one-hundred-dollar starting capital into a bankroll of $11,000.00 in three weeks' time using 10% of available capital on a wildcat place selection method. Admittedly, the place procedure was highly suspect, if not downright unsound, but I just happened to catch it in a successful cycle.

There was a bird I used to know in California who preferred to take his action at Las Vegas, between "lost weekends." He had more than one major track there from which to select his action. He was strictly a win bettor, and used $2\frac{1}{2}\%$ of available capital as his control. This always seemed low to me, reflecting lack of confidence in his own ability as a selector. Five percent of available capital should be quite safe for a good handicapper-analyst, or an operator with a sound system for selecting win plays.

Here's how it works in practice. We'll run off a few plays from the selections we made for the handicap-analysis chapter.

Starting with a capital of $100 and using 5% as our control, our wager on Mark's Puzzle would then be $5.00. Our return for the $7.50 payoff is $18.50 and our net profit, $13.50. This is added to the bankroll making it stand at $113.50. Five percent of this new amount is $5.65, which is closer to six dollars than five, so our next wager, on Kismiss, is $6.00.

This one we blew, reducing our capital to $107.50, but we do not regress in our betting. We remain on $6.00 flat bets until such time as a winner and/or winners build our capital to a new high, 5% of which would require *raising* the wager. So we had $6.00 on Edliss in the third, which paid $5.20. The gross return, $15.60. Net, $9.60. New capital high, $117.10. Five percent still calls for a six-dollar bet.

My Friend saved only the place, so our capital shrinks to $111.10, and the $3.50 we got on Tocsin didn't improve it too much. The capital stood at $115.60 and the bet still at $6.00 going into the sixth, where Deep Breath converted for $8.00. Our capital takes a jump to $133.50 and the bet moves up to seven dollars, which is played, to win, on Summer Tan. The $4.10 mutuel nets us $7.35, and a new high for the bankroll, $140.95. Five percent of this is still $7.00, which is played on Voyante.

Voyante's $27.90 payoff nets us $80.65 and our nest egg now rests at $221.60. Our bet moves up to $11.00. This amount we lose on Billy's Gem in the ninth, for he was only able to save the Show. Our capital at the end of the day's run, $210.60. The eleven-dollar bet would be carried forward to Big Billie in the first race on the following day, who paid $22.10. And so on and up.

Let's take these same selections and see what happened with a 10% place play. The procedure is the same as above except that we use ten percent of available capital instead of five. Our bets could increase from ten dollars to a thousand, but we'd still be using only 10% of available capital. It is possible to use this with the regression feature, of course, though I personally don't like regression. The theory here, is that by letting bets rise and fall with wins and losses that one could never go broke no matter how long a sustained run of losers he encountered, since he would never be betting more than ten percent of the remaining capital after each loss.

There can be no question about this being an added safety factor, but I do not like to retreat. I'd rather stand on flat bets during a losing period and be in a position to get a full measure of profit when I do get a winner. To me there is something negative about backing up simply because you sustain a loss or two, then when a hit comes, to be on such a reduced wager that the resultant come-back seems weak. So, I never use the regression feature. Just thought I'd mention it. The decision is yours, to use it or not to use it.

So, on this day, we had only one loser in the place category and the build-up was more startling than with win play. At the end of the eighth race our capital stood at $331.55, and the bet going into the ninth, which we lost, was $33.00, leaving us with a total operating capital of $298.55 and a bet of $33.00 still, to start the next day. This was, of course, Big Billie, and the place payoff, $12.70. If this interests you, go on run the action out yourself to gain facility in handling it.

For show play, the percentage could be raised somewhat and still keep within safety bounds, but I recommend it be left at 10%. The build up will be only slightly slower, and the conservative operator will be willing to consider that payment for the added safety factor.

There was no loss in the show slot on this first day of February, so that the show build-up was only about sixteen dollars less than on the win end. From $100.00 the capital built to $194.35 in just one day's show action.

That should give the student-fan a pretty fair idea of the potential of this method of money control. I hardly need point out that it's a powerhouse. The rate of build-up—straight, place, or show—will be in direct proportion to your ability as a selector. And you should be getting pretty handy at it by now.

There is still another kind of money action which has considerable merit. This is known as Due Column Control. It is of especial value where wagering on more than one horse to win per race, and not relying on any one winner to resolve the series. It can, however, be used effectively when backing only one horse per race.

You decide in advance to pay yourself a certain minimum wage for the effort of being at the track and placing the wagers. A gradual progression is used, not the destructive doubling up kind, without regard to odds. Thus, you may get a number of winners along the line of action without clearing your Due Column which builds up with each race until the point is reached where you get a winner with sufficiently large mutuel to give you a plus amount equal to or greater than the amount called out in your Due Column at that point. The series is then complete, and play starts over again.

Here's how your work sheet will look, using Clocker's selections at Gulfstream Park on March 11, 1957:

DATE	RACE	HORSE	BET	DUE	MUTUEL	MINUS	PLUS
3/1	1	Night Tears	$2				
	1	Tillie Temple	2				
	1	Revolark	2	$ 3	$ 7.10		$ 1.10
	2	False Pride	2				
	2	Free And Busy	2				
	2	Untimely	2	$ 6		$ 4.90	
	3	Willie Ratner	2				
	3	French Coat	2				
	3	Stratmat	2	$ 9	$14.80		$ 3.10
3/1	4	Chateau	$2				
	4	Man Of Quest	2				
	4	Charier	2	$12		$ 2.90	
	5	War Command	2		$ 7.80		
	5	Fleet Peet	4				
	5	Good Gesture	4	$15		$ 5.10	
	6	Ratheram	4				
	6	Rock Castle	4				
	6	Homeplace	4	$18		$17.10	
	7	Tussle Patch	4				
	7	Admiral Vee	4		$ 8.50		
	7	Chit Chat	4	$21		$12.10	
	8	Indac	5				
	8	Big Mister	5				
	8	Dance Nsing	5	*$24*	$26.20		*$38.40*

(This completes this series as the PLUS Column of $38.40 is

greater than our DUE Column requirement which is only $24.00 at this point. We start over with $2 bets.)

9	Ardan Lark	2		
9	Blimey	2		$20.80
9	SCRATCHED	0	*$ 3*	*$16.80*

(This is also complete since PLUS Column is $16.80 and only $3.00 is DUE.)

So, by playing multiple ready-made pix, and riding along on a slow progression, we caught four winners, from which our Due Column Control gave us a net profit of $55.20.

Had we played these same pix on a $2.00 flat bet straight through, our profit would have been but $11.30. The fact that there *was* a flat bet profit made it possible to use a progression to very good advantage.

There are two things to remember about progressions. 1) You cannot force, by progression, a profit from a selection method which will not produce a flat-bet profit. Sooner or later the adverse percentage will get you. 2) It always requires a larger operating capital to carry through a progression than it does to play the same selections on a flat-bet basis. In other words, when you make the weight of your money do the work, though your profit will be greater in actual cash, the yield from total money invested (percentage of yield, that is) will be less from progression over a period of time, than from flat betting. But when a man's in a hurry, he's usually willing to spend a little more to get there. So I'm not going to tell you to do this or that. Your choice should be predicated on your circumstances and your goal. If you're in a hurry, and have the bankroll, by all means use one of these tried and true methods. But avoid those destructive doubling-up progressions like the plague. They look fine in theory, but believe me, they'll squash you flatter than a bug.

The feature which saves the Due Column Control from becoming destructive (mild though it is, it *is* a straight progression we used) is the fact that we're getting winners all along the line, even though many of them are bound to be short-priced. Even these short ones, however, have their function in this system. They tend to hold the Minus Column within bounds so that we're poised and ready to clear our Due Column when a fair-to-middlin' longshot converts for us.

20. The Willing-Hoss System

Here's one for the system player who wants something a little different. This one, we developed during the spring racing of 1955 at Balmoral-Arlington Park, which is part of the Chicago circuit. It's still a good wrinkle and we'll use the original workout from which this system was tested.

In one sense, this is a present form system, though actually what we hope to point up with our rule is that the nag must not only have ability but must show a willingness to run up with the forward echelon. Many thoroughbreds have ability. Not so many of them show much willingness to extend themselves.

To locate his contenders, all that will be required of the operator is a bit of simple addition. The resulting figure will represent not only the horse's ability but his willingness to compete. Those beetles that plod along, making like tail-end Charlie, way back yonder behind the pace, are a bad risk even if they do occasionally seem to come charging down the stretch out of nowhere to rack up a win. There can be no question that this type of contestant can be an excitement producer par excellence. It's a real thrill to watch him operate, but it's mighty hard on the pocketbook.

By backing a willing-type hoss, as defined for the purpose

of this system, we have one that is at least in the forward flight and therefore in a position to win if he has the ability to do so. That come-from-behinder has to rely on all those horses ahead of him running out of gas when they hit the stretch.

In pursuing this willingness idea, we found the manner in which a beastie finished a race (unlike the out-of-the-clouds variety) was not as significant as the way he raced before the finish, so we decided to eliminate the finish from consideration. In fact, if our qualifier finished badly, we have all the better chance of getting a price today. The average fan cannot resist a horse that won or ran in-the-money on his last trip.

So, we decided to concentrate on the first three "calls" in the past performances for our information. And we found that the information that was pertinent was not so much the hide's actual running position with regard to the other contestants, but the number of lengths off the pace. In other words, it didn't matter too much if the horse was running one, two or eleven at these calls provided that, if he wasn't himself setting the pace (leading), he wasn't too far off of it. To avoid complicating the thing by setting maximum allowable lengths off the pace at each of these first three "calls" and to try to compensate for possible bumping or other traffic mishaps which might make one call look bad, we decided what we needed was an average picture of the early running. To get this, we added together the number of lengths off the pace on each of these three calls. If he was leading at one or more of these calls it was regarded as a zero for that (or those) call(s).

To illustrate, let's suppose that we're looking at the last race of a horse that was running fifth, *four lengths* off the pace at the first call; first by one at the pre-stretch (second) call; and sixth by 1½ at the in-stretch (third) call. Since he was setting the pace at the pre-stretch call, we regard this as zero (0), and add together the lengths behind the leader in the first call, which was four, and the in-stretch call, which was 1½. Our willingness figure for this hypothetical contender would then be 6½.

By trial and error we established that the number of lengths beyond ten (10) was not significant. Thus our contenders in any race became those whose total number of lengths off the pace was 10 or less. Our hypothetical nag, then, with only 6½ points would qualify.

It was found further that simply because one of these contenders had a figure of two and another a figure of nine it did not follow that the one with the two was a better bet than the one with nine, or the one with all zero calls (leading at all three calls) was necessarily a more likely winner than the one with the ten, which was the maximum allowed for contention. Too often the contestant with ten had simply been out in tougher competition, or had encountered trouble.

Our band of contenders, qualified on willingness, must necessarily vary from race to race. In some races there will be but one, and in others none. But most usually, we will find ourselves with two or more qualified contenders which will face us with a small separation problem. This can be handled in this way.

1) If the race is a claimer, qualify the contender for play which showed his willingness at the highest claiming tag. If he was in contention in a $4,000 claimer, let's say, and the others showed their willingness in $3,500 races, the one qualified as a contender off of the $4,000 race will be given the nod.

2) If the race is an allowance (even you system players should read the secretary's conditions, remember), the ultimate selection shall have been qualified as a contender off of a stake of one kind or another, viz., AlwS, ScwS, WfaS, HcpS, etc.

3) If the race is a maiden affair, the final selection should have shown his willingness in an Alw, a stake, or an AlwM.

We would not assume that a claiming tag, even a high-grade claimer, was superior to a maiden designation. We would be more nearly right in assuming that the maiden designation was better, since the owner had never risked losing him to a halter man and therefore considered him too valuable to enter in a claiming race.

4) For the feature races, which are stakes or big name handicaps, best bet is to go get a hot dog and concentrate on the next race. However, separation can be attempted on the basis of choosing the contender showing the most Stakes in his past performances.

No effort was made to separate horses still tied after applying our class angle, that is, those races in which there was no clearly defined class edge. I take that back. I did fudge one race for the workout to see what would happen. This was Night Intruder, in the first race on June 3rd. I went to the second race back when I failed to get a separation by comparing qualifying races. By fudging back to the previous race, I was able to qualify Night Intruder off of a stake. But this, actually, was a case where a mere glance made it clear he was the class of the entire field. However, it is an idea you might use if you require more action than obtained in the accompanying Workout.

One hundred twenty-two plays in a month should be ample action to suit most, however. Of these, thirty-four won, giving a win figure of 28%. This is more than satisfactory considering the average win mutuel of $11.24, and a yield on total invested capital of 56.6%. By beating the price, we once again beat the percentages, and thus the races.

Balmoral & Arlington at Washington Park					June, 1955
DATE	RACE	HORSE	WIN	PLACE	SHOW
6/1	1	Black Poppy	$27.80	$ 8.20	$ 4.40
	2	Bleu Feature	8.20	3.80	3.20

DATE	RACE	HORSE	WIN	PLACE	SHOW
	4	Sir Lari	34.20	21.40	13.60
	5	Demaree	. . .	. . .	3.20
	6	Top Traffic	5.00	3.40	2.40
	7	Blue Choir	3.80	2.60	3.00
	8	Sir Tribal	7.60	3.60	2.60
6/2	1	Neal Elyse	6.00	3.60	2.40
	2	Kentucky Kid	3.60	2.60	2.40
	3	Guard Rail	3.40	2.60	2.20
	5	Pussy Cat	6.00	3.40	2.60
	6	Torch Of War	. . .	. . .	. . .
	7	Killimor	. . .	. . .	. . .
	8	By Gone Days	. . .	. . .	. . .
6/3	1	Night Intruder	6.00	3.60	2.40
	3	Fauroyal	. . .	5.20	3.40
	7	Olympia Lou	. . .	. . .	. . .
	8	Sky Maid	. . .	. . .	. . .
6/4	2	Hottentot	. . .	. . .	. . .
	3	Skippy's First	. . .	. . .	. . .
	7	Insouciant	. . .	. . .	. . .
	8	Arete	19.40	8.80	5.80
	9	Great Regret	. . .	. . .	. . .
6/6	3	Know All	$ 6.00	$ 4.20	$ 3.60
	4	Lucky Jonnie	. . .	. . .	. . .
	5	Lady Elliott	6.40	3.60	3.00
	6	Breakers	. . .	3.00	2.40
	7	Parklea	. . .	. . .	. . .
	8	Passing Hour	. . .	. . .	. . .
6/7	2	Sixty-Two	. . .	. . .	. . .
	4	Grecian Ayr	. . .	. . .	2.20
	5	Dream Pattern	. . .	. . .	5.80
	6	Mayo Lady	. . .	. . .	5.20
	7	Russell TS	. . .	6.00	4.60
	8	Bobtail Willie	. . .	8.00	6.40
6/8	3	Skippy's First	4.60	3.60	2.80
	5	Royal Bred	17.40	7.00	4.60
	6	Alternative	. . .	. . .	4.00
	8	Roman Senator	11.20	5.40	3.40
6/9	1	Le Sabre	. . .	. . .	. . .

DATE	RACE	HORSE	WIN	PLACE	SHOW
	3	Corona Lark	. . .	. . .	. . .
	4	Big Step	. . .	. . .	. . .
	5	Intelligent	. . .	. . .	. . .
	7	Fair Song	21.20	10.60	5.80
	8	Blue Fay	. . .	. . .	. . .
6/10	1	Moose Sign	4.80	3.40	2.80
	4	Mrs. Sweeney	. . .	. . .	. . .
	5	Baby's Pal	$ . . .	$ . . .	$ 3.00
	7	Morse Flash	. . .	. . .	. . .
6/11	2	Fleet Dream	. . .	. . .	. . .
	4	Snorkel	. . .	. . .	. . .
6/13	1	Jolly Well	. . .	. . .	. . .
	3	Hy Apache	. . .	. . .	. . .
	5	Stroller	17.20	7.80	4.40
	6	Pasatiempo	. . .	2.80	2.40
	7	Bobtag	9.80	4.20	2.80
	8	Tattenham	. . .	. . .	2.80
6/14	1	Morse Flash	. . .	. . .	. . .
	4	Gorgeous Miss	. . .	2.40	2.40
	5	Flying Record	. . .	. . .	6.00
	7	Free Too	. . .	. . .	. . .
6/15	2	Hi Sky	. . .	. . .	. . .
	4	Sky Capers	10.20	5.80	4.40
	5	Dance Nsing	3.60	2.80	2.40
	8	Attavar	. . .	. . .	. . .
6/16	1	On Stanley On	. . .	. . .	. . .
	2	Scairt Rabbit	. . .	. . .	. . .
	3	Iwillifican	17.80	7.40	5.40
	4	Ardansgal	. . .	. . .	. . .
	5	Maybe Mabel	. . .	. . .	. . .
	7	Cosentina	. . .	2.80	2.20
	9	Alfred Boulder	8.20	6.60	4.40
6/17	1	King Mustang	$ . . .	$ . . .	$ . . .
	2	Educt	. . .	6.00	4.00
	3	Jacalu	13.20	6.80	4.80
	4	Pastoral	. . .	. . .	3.00
	5	O'Troon	. . .	. . .	. . .
	7	Direct North	. . .	. . .	. . .

DATE	RACE	HORSE	WIN	PLACE	SHOW
	8	Romango	. . .	. . .	. . .
6/18	2	Ari's Setup	. . .	. . .	3.60
	8	Vidi	11.80	5.80	4.20
	9	Bonnie Inez	. . .	. . .	. . .
6/20	1	Mighty Tom	. . .	. . .	. . .
	2	Kiami	. . .	4.20	3.20
	8	Alternative	. . .	. . .	3.80
	9	Agreed	. . .	. . .	9.00
6/21	2	Get For Home	. . .	. . .	5.20
	8	Feud	. . .	. . .	. . .
6/22	2	Arete	11.60	3.80	3.00
	4	Betsy T.	. . .	. . .	. . .
	7	Nimble Doll	. . .	. . .	2.80
	8	Vasco Da Gama	. . .	. . .	. . .
	9	Queen's Regret	. . .	. . .	. . .
6/23	2	Mahmoud Relic	. . .	. . .	. . .
	4	Patill	. . .	. . .	. . .
	5	Intelligent	. . .	. . .	. . .
	7	Angel's Doll	. . .	12.40	7.20
	8	Sandy M.	$15.60	$ 8.00	$ 5.20
6/24	2	Sherry L.	. . .	. . .	. . .
	4	Kentucky Kid	15.80	6.40	4.40
	5	Restraint	. . .	. . .	. . .
	6	Baby Tucky	. . .	. . .	. . .
	8	Pastoral	. . .	. . .	. . .
6/25	1	Shifty Dora	. . .	. . .	. . .
	2	Andy B. W.	. . .	. . .	. . .
	4	Heart Flash	. . .	. . .	. . .
	6	Lori-Jane	. . .	. . .	4.00
	8	Black Widow	. . .	. . .	. . .
6/27	1	Corona Lark	. . .	10.40	7.40
	2	Whitted	. . .	. . .	. . .
	5	Miss Energy	. . .	. . .	. . .
	8	Jumbo Lies	. . .	. . .	. . .
6/28	1	Shano	9.00	5.40	2.60
	2	Is Yours	. . .	. . .	. . .
	4	Skeptical Kid	12.20	4.60	3.20
6/29	2	Witch Way	5.80	4.00	3.00

DATE	RACE	HORSE	WIN	PLACE	SHOW
	4	Recline	. . .	2.40	2.40
	8	Tall Iris	. . .	. . .	. . .
6/30	1	Moose Sign	. . .	. . .	. . .
	2	Ritas Flyer	17.40	7.00	4.80
	3	Wing-Two	. . .	. . .	. . .
	4	Medico	. . .	. . .	4.40

Though the place and show each showed a small profit, this shaped up as a win system. So if you like this easy way of selecting and can wait for your prices, just remember there's many a hard bitten professional speculator who doesn't earn 56.6% on his total invested capital. But you can bet the bottom of your pocket he likes what he is doing. It suits his temperament, and he's willing to settle for maybe as low as 3% yield in some cases for his peace and security.

21. Angles

No book on turf speculation can be entirely complete without a discussion of angles and angle players.

The angle player is neither a handicap-analyst nor a system player, and yet he is a little of both. He is essentially a spot player and he has certain definite patterns that must show up before he has a play. The more different angles he has to watch for, the more action he can expect to get, but many of them use just the one pet angle which may show up only once in a blue moon.

Some of the angles one runs across border on the psychotic. Others, though cut-to-the-bone short cuts, are based on sound ideas.

An example of the zany kind, which I can hardly recommend, is the "bird-watcher" angle. The operator of this one must wait for his cue from our feathered friends. If a bird, or a flight of birds, should happen to wheel across the finish line before post time, the angle player has a spot. If there is only one bird, he plays number-one post position. If it is a flight of birds, he counts them and plays that number. I suppose, lacking birds to give him the divine tip-off he could, in an emergency, resort to butterflies, or even horse flies.

Let's take a look at a few of them which seem to have a modicum of common sense behind them:

1) The "horses that beat each other" angle, which we mentioned earlier in the text. It is a good one and certainly appears based on sound reasoning. The operator has a spot when he finds two horses in the same race that have met recently and, preferably, ran first and second in that previous race. He notes the weights they each carried in that previous meeting and compares them with the weight assignments today. If there has been a weight-shift favoring the horse that ran second last time, he is the play today. If the same weight differential exists today as in the previous race, the angle player takes the previous winner to repeat.

2) L.S. angle. This long shot angle requires a cursory perusal of the past performances. It is predicated on an *increase* in weight. To be a L.S. spot, the horse must have looked terrible in his last two races, finishing ten or more lengths down the track in each. BUT, instead of getting weight off under the conditions, for his poor showings, he is being brought back today at a higher impost than he carried in either of those previous bad races.

Crazy? Let's see what's behind it. Those last two races certainly don't show it, but let's say the trainer knows his horse has come to hand as a result of the tightening he got in these two, or maybe the last one. There are other ways for a horseman to judge sharp form than the manner in which his horse finished recently. So he's anxious to capitalize on this sharp edge. He takes the first race in the condition book in which his horse will fit. He may even have selected it *because* of the high impost his horse will have to carry, knowing the animal to be a good weight-packer when sharp. And those two bad races *plus* a boost in weight should keep the two-buck bettors off in droves, hence an even better longshot price. Enough of them get home free at fancy mutuels to substantiate this reasoning.

3) The straw poll angle. This is a tote board angle, but

requires a little advance spade work. The operator may work up a consensus which could include the *Racing Form* Consensus and the local newspaper consensus and the Morning Line at the track where he's holding forth. He marks these Consensus horses on his program as "A," "B," and "C," the top-figure horse being "A," the second-figure horse "B" and the third figure horse "C." So fortified, he is ready to take his straw poll. He simply stands close enough to a win mutuel window so as to be able to hear the numbers called out as the bettors back their hunches or their judgement, or as they do in most cases, the Consensus of opinion of the public selectors.

Every time the operator hears a number called out he marks a vote opposite the horses name in pencil. He continues this until he has a hundred votes. Then he knocks it off and figures the odds each of these horses should be on the board according to the vote he has taken. If one of these horses is bet substantially below what his straw poll indicates it should be, then he concludes a gob of smart money has been bet on this played-down nag, probably through the $100 window, which is never used in taking the straw poll. If his straw vote agrees substantially with the tote board, he concludes the odds are being made by the two-buck bettor, who is a notorious follower of Consensus opinion, hence no smart money is involved and there is no play for him. But if he finds the kind of underplay mentioned above, he goes along with the smart money, but he plays to place, for the smart money, he figures, is stable money, and stable money is notoriously premature . . . as far as the win end is concerned. It seems as though the boys around the barns just can't wait. They live in dread that their sharpening horse might "run in" on them, and catch them without so much as a deuce going.

This impatience is so prevalent that I knew a chap in California who never played stable tips when given, and he had some pretty good connections. He wrote them down in his little black book, and played them the *next* time they started. To the best of my knowledge, he made out very well.

4) Here is another consensus-tote board angle. In this one, the operator observes the tote board about five minutes before post time, or three minutes if that allows him enough time to make his purchase in the event a play materializes. If the top Consensus selection in the *Form* is *not* favored in the betting, he plays it to win.

The logic behind this? It is the angle player's way of getting the percentages working with him by beating the price on a horse already pointed up as best by five of the country's leading public selectors. Ordinarily this horse would be underlaid by virtue of being a Consensus selection. If the public's attention is diverted away from this horse, he can get a fair price on it if it wins. He may even get an overlay.

5) Here's another smart-money angle, though not a long shot play this time. Here again, the player must wait till the last minute or two or three—whatever he needs to get to the mutuel window and transact his business. With this one also he makes use of the consensus. If the bet favorite is *not* one of the three horses mentioned in the consensus, the operator concludes smart money is responsible and he goes along . . . to place.

6) Disqualification angle. This player has to have patience for there aren't too many of these spots. He has a play only when he finds a horse that won his last race but was disqualified and deprived of the win purse. The idea here is that the trainer will do everything in his power to hold the horse together until he can send him out again to collect a purse to replace the one snatched from his grasp last time. Whether this is the answer, or whether it is simply a case of a sharp horse retaining his edge long enough to repeat a winning effort, they do seem to bang right back with surprising regular-

ity. At least that is my impression from more or less casual observation of this angle. I do not, however, have a long workout on this one to back up my impression.

We'll let you do that, if you're the angle player type, and if this angle appeals to you.

There are many, many more angles, just as there are countless systems, some of which are good, some indifferent, and some plain lousy. I believe these six are the best of their kind. You're welcome to them for what they're worth to you.

A lot of fans are happier with a half-dozen or so angles to watch for than they could be with the finest single system extant. It's a question of temperament. Who can say which type of player has the best of it? The handicap-analyst? The system player? The angle player?

Sure, I have an opinion, but it's biased because I am, myself, an analyst. Let's look at it this way. Any way you, the student-fan, can make an honest buck off the beetles is best —for you.

So if you have not already made up your mind, go back and read this book again. The human animal learns through repetition—and by doing. So, when you settle on what you want, run off your on-paper check. Work at it until you have confidence not only in the procedure but in your own ability to handle it. Then, and only then, has the time come for you to back your decisions with money, marbles, or chalk.

22. It Wasn't Rigged

Early in this book we said we'd have some more to say about the phenomenal growth in popularity of thoroughbred racing in recent years—why it has now become one of the billion-dollar industries.

Anything as lush as that is a natural target for the larcenous brotherhood—or was not too many years ago. But things have changed. The fast buck artists have learned there are easier ways to make a nefarious living than "rigging" horse races. This came about when the racing fraternity finally realized that if racing was to survive, it must have the confidence of the two-buck bettor.

Without his support, racing was doomed. For the track managements, the horsemen, and the horses themselves are merely actors and stage hands in the pageant. Each and every one of them is dependent on the acceptance and support of Joe Racing Fan.

Consequently, once this fact was recognized, one of the most conscientious drives in the history of American enterprise was launched to eliminate the undesirables and to banish once and for all the unfair and dishonest practices.

Reforms resulted. The photo finish camera; the automatic

starting gate; stringent rules and regulations with drastic punishments for violation; the film patrol which is a movie of the running of each race; saliva and urine tests to discourage stimulation or doping; lip tattooing to prevent the use of "ringers"; and many, many more.

Hollywood Park, at Inglewood, California, was the pacesetter in gaining and holding the public confidence. The progressive, far-seeing pattern set by the management of this track has been the blueprint for reforms at the other plants.

Wendell Cassidy, a Hollywood Park steward, believes the "rigged race" is no longer possible. He speaks with authority as he is also the head of the Performance Analysis Department at the Inglewood Oval.

"We know now," he says, "substantially all that can be learned about the running habits and ability of the horses at our track. The motion pictures and our performance analysis show up anything unusual or contrary to the running pattern of a horse. We know from our records just how a horse breaks from the gate, how he hits the pace, when and where he generally makes his move, his favorite distance, and the style of riding that suits him best. If the pattern is perceptibly changed, *we investigate*. When a horse runs contrary to his established performances and what is normally expected of him, for no apparent reason, we make it a point to find out why. There is a reason for everything that happens in racing, and the motion pictures and the performance analysis recordings tell us what *does* happen."

There is no room for cheating in a set-up like this. If it is tried, the guilty party is quickly spotted and dealt with.

So there's no need to spend your time crook-hunting. That department is in competent hands, leaving you free to spend your time making the very best selections you are capable of.

Good hunting.

MELVIN POWERS SELF-IMPROVEMENT LIBRARY

ASTROLOGY

BRIDGE

BUSINESS, STUDY & REFERENCE

CALLIGRAPHY

CHESS & CHECKERS

COOKERY & HERBS

__ CULPEPER'S HERBAL REMEDIES *Dr. Nicholas Culpeper*	3.00
__ FAST GOURMET COOKBOOK *Poppy Cannon*	2.50
__ GINSENG The Myth & The Truth *Joseph P. Hou*	3.00
__ HEALING POWER OF HERBS *May Bethel*	4.00
__ HEALING POWER OF NATURAL FOODS *May Bethel*	3.00
__ HERB HANDBOOK *Dawn MacLeod*	3.00
__ HERBS FOR COOKING AND HEALING *Dr. Donald Law*	2.00
__ HERBS FOR HEALTH—How to Grow & Use Them *Louise Evans Doole*	4.00
__ HOME GARDEN COOKBOOK—Delicious Natural Food Recipes *Ken Kraft*	3.00
__ MEDICAL HERBALIST *edited by Dr. J. R. Yemm*	3.00
__ NATURAL FOOD COOKBOOK *Dr. Harry C. Bond*	3.00
__ NATURE'S MEDICINES *Richard Lucas*	3.00
__ VEGETABLE GARDENING FOR BEGINNERS *Hugh Wiberg*	2.00
__ VEGETABLES FOR TODAY'S GARDENS *R. Milton Carleton*	2.00
__ VEGETARIAN COOKERY *Janet Walker*	4.00
__ VEGETARIAN COOKING MADE EASY & DELECTABLE *Veronica Vezza*	3.00
__ VEGETARIAN DELIGHTS—A Happy Cookbook for Health *K. R. Mehta*	2.00
__ VEGETARIAN GOURMET COOKBOOK *Joyce McKinnel*	3.00

GAMBLING & POKER

__ ADVANCED POKER STRATEGY & WINNING PLAY *A. D. Livingston*	5.00
__ HOW NOT TO LOSE AT POKER *Jeffrey Lloyd Castle*	3.00
__ HOW TO WIN AT DICE GAMES *Skip Frey*	3.00
__ HOW TO WIN AT POKER *Terence Reese & Anthony T. Watkins*	5.00
__ SECRETS OF WINNING POKER *George S. Coffin*	3.00
__ WINNING AT CRAPS *Dr. Lloyd T. Commins*	4.00
__ WINNING AT GIN *Chester Wander & Cy Rice*	3.00
__ WINNING AT POKER—An Expert's Guide *John Archer*	5.00
__ WINNING AT 21—An Expert's Guide *John Archer*	5.00
__ WINNING POKER SYSTEMS *Norman Zadeh*	3.00

HEALTH

__ BEE POLLEN *Lynda Lyngheim & Jack Scagnetti*	3.00
__ DR. LINDNER'S SPECIAL WEIGHT CONTROL METHOD *P. G. Lindner, M.D.*	2.00
__ HELP YOURSELF TO BETTER SIGHT *Margaret Darst Corbett*	3.00
__ HOW TO IMPROVE YOUR VISION *Dr. Robert A. Kraskin*	3.00
__ HOW YOU CAN STOP SMOKING PERMANENTLY *Ernest Caldwell*	3.00
__ MIND OVER PLATTER *Peter G. Lindner, M.D.*	3.00
__ NATURE'S WAY TO NUTRITION & VIBRANT HEALTH *Robert J. Scrutton*	3.00
__ NEW CARBOHYDRATE DIET COUNTER *Patti Lopez-Pereira*	2.00
__ QUICK & EASY EXERCISES FOR FACIAL BEAUTY *Judy Smith-deal*	2.00
__ QUICK & EASY EXERCISES FOR FIGURE BEAUTY *Judy Smith-deal*	2.00
__ REFLEXOLOGY *Dr. Maybelle Segal*	3.00
__ REFLEXOLOGY FOR GOOD HEALTH *Anna Kaye & Don C. Matchan*	3.00
__ 30 DAYS TO BEAUTIFUL LEGS *Dr. Marc Selner*	3.00
__ YOU CAN LEARN TO RELAX *Dr. Samuel Gutwirth*	3.00
__ YOUR ALLERGY—What To Do About It *Allan Knight, M.D.*	3.00

HOBBIES

__ BEACHCOMBING FOR BEGINNERS *Norman Hickin*	2.00
__ BLACKSTONE'S MODERN CARD TRICKS *Harry Blackstone*	3.00
__ BLACKSTONE'S SECRETS OF MAGIC *Harry Blackstone*	3.00
__ COIN COLLECTING FOR BEGINNERS *Burton Hobson & Fred Reinfeld*	3.00
__ ENTERTAINING WITH ESP *Tony 'Doc' Shiels*	2.00
__ 400 FASCINATING MAGIC TRICKS YOU CAN DO *Howard Thurston*	4.00
__ HOW I TURN JUNK INTO FUN AND PROFIT *Sari*	3.00
__ HOW TO WRITE A HIT SONG & SELL IT *Tommy Boyce*	7.00
__ JUGGLING MADE EASY *Rudolf Dittrich*	3.00
__ MAGIC FOR ALL AGES *Walter Gibson*	4.00
__ MAGIC MADE EASY *Byron Wels*	2.00
__ STAMP COLLECTING FOR BEGINNERS *Burton Hobson*	3.00

HORSE PLAYERS' WINNING GUIDES

__ BETTING HORSES TO WIN *Les Conklin*	3.00

MARRIAGE, SEX & PARENTHOOD

___ ABILITY TO LOVE *Dr. Allan Fromme*	5.00
___ ENCYCLOPEDIA OF MODERN SEX & LOVE TECHNIQUES *Macandrew*	5.00
___ GUIDE TO SUCCESSFUL MARRIAGE *Drs. Albert Ellis & Robert Harper*	5.00
___ HOW TO RAISE AN EMOTIONALLY HEALTHY, HAPPY CHILD *A. Ellis*	4.00
___ SEX WITHOUT GUILT *Albert Ellis, Ph.D.*	5.00
___ SEXUALLY ADEQUATE MALE *Frank S. Caprio, M.D.*	3.00
___ SEXUALLY FULFILLED MAN *Dr. Rachel Copelan*	5.00

MELVIN POWERS' MAIL ORDER LIBRARY

___ HOW TO GET RICH IN MAIL ORDER *Melvin Powers*	15.00
___ HOW TO WRITE A GOOD ADVERTISEMENT *Victor O. Schwab*	15.00
___ MAIL ORDER MADE EASY *J. Frank Brumbaugh*	10.00
___ U.S. MAIL ORDER SHOPPER'S GUIDE *Susan Spitzer*	10.00

METAPHYSICS & OCCULT

___ BOOK OF TALISMANS, AMULETS & ZODIACAL GEMS *William Pavitt*	5.00
___ CONCENTRATION—A Guide to Mental Mastery *Mouni Sadhu*	4.00
___ CRITIQUES OF GOD *Edited by Peter Angeles*	7.00
___ EXTRA-TERRESTRIAL INTELLIGENCE—The First Encounter	6.00
___ FORTUNE TELLING WITH CARDS *P. Foli*	4.00
___ HANDWRITING ANALYSIS MADE EASY *John Marley*	4.00
___ HANDWRITING TELLS *Nadya Olyanova*	5.00
___ HOW TO INTERPRET DREAMS, OMENS & FORTUNE TELLING SIGNS *Gettings*	3.00
___ HOW TO UNDERSTAND YOUR DREAMS *Geoffrey A. Dudley*	3.00
___ ILLUSTRATED YOGA *William Zorn*	3.00
___ IN DAYS OF GREAT PEACE *Mouni Sadhu*	3.00
___ LSD—THE AGE OF MIND *Bernard Roseman*	2.00
___ MAGICIAN—His Training and Work *W. E. Butler*	3.00
___ MEDITATION *Mouni Sadhu*	5.00
___ MODERN NUMEROLOGY *Morris C. Goodman*	3.00
___ NUMEROLOGY—ITS FACTS AND SECRETS *Ariel Yvon Taylor*	3.00
___ NUMEROLOGY MADE EASY *W. Mykian*	4.00
___ PALMISTRY MADE EASY *Fred Gettings*	3.00
___ PALMISTRY MADE PRACTICAL *Elizabeth Daniels Squire*	4.00
___ PALMISTRY SECRETS REVEALED *Henry Frith*	3.00
___ PROPHECY IN OUR TIME *Martin Ebon*	2.50
___ PSYCHOLOGY OF HANDWRITING *Nadya Olyanova*	5.00
___ SUPERSTITION—Are You Superstitious? *Eric Maple*	2.00
___ TAROT *Mouni Sadhu*	6.00
___ TAROT OF THE BOHEMIANS *Papus*	5.00
___ WAYS TO SELF-REALIZATION *Mouni Sadhu*	3.00
___ WHAT YOUR HANDWRITING REVEALS *Albert E. Hughes*	3.00
___ WITCHCRAFT, MAGIC & OCCULTISM—A Fascinating History *W. B. Crow*	5.00
___ WITCHCRAFT—THE SIXTH SENSE *Justine Glass*	5.00
___ WORLD OF PSYCHIC RESEARCH *Hereward Carrington*	2.00

SELF-HELP & INSPIRATIONAL

___ DAILY POWER FOR JOYFUL LIVING *Dr. Donald Curtis*	5.00
___ DYNAMIC THINKING *Melvin Powers*	2.00
___ EXUBERANCE—Your Guide to Happiness & Fulfillment *Dr. Paul Kurtz*	3.00
___ GREATEST POWER IN THE UNIVERSE *U. S. Andersen*	5.00
___ GROW RICH WHILE YOU SLEEP *Ben Sweetland*	3.00
___ GROWTH THROUGH REASON *Albert Ellis, Ph.D.*	4.00
___ GUIDE TO PERSONAL HAPPINESS *Albert Ellis, Ph.D. & Irving Becker, Ed. D.*	5.00
___ HELPING YOURSELF WITH APPLIED PSYCHOLOGY *R. Henderson*	2.00
___ HELPING YOURSELF WITH PSYCHIATRY *Frank S. Caprio, M.D.*	2.00
___ HOW TO ATTRACT GOOD LUCK *A. H. Z. Carr*	4.00
___ HOW TO DEVELOP A WINNING PERSONALITY *Martin Panzer*	5.00
___ HOW TO DEVELOP AN EXCEPTIONAL MEMORY *Young & Gibson*	4.00
___ HOW TO LIVE WITH A NEUROTIC *Albert Ellis, Ph. D.*	5.00
___ HOW TO OVERCOME YOUR FEARS *M. P. Leahy, M.D.*	3.00
___ HOW YOU CAN HAVE CONFIDENCE AND POWER *Les Giblin*	5.00
___ HUMAN PROBLEMS & HOW TO SOLVE THEM *Dr. Donald Curtis*	5.00
___ I CAN *Ben Sweetland*	5.00